Wargaming in History

Series Editor
Stuart Asquith

The American Civil War

• • • • •

Paul Stevenson

 Sterling Publishing Co., Inc.   New York

Published in 1990 by Sterling Publishing Company, Inc.
387 Park Avenue South, New York, N.Y. 10016

Distributed in Canada by Sterling Publishing
c/o Canadian Manda Group, P.O. Box 920, Station U
Toronto, Ontario, Canada M8Z 5P9

© 1990 by Argus Books

ISBN 0-8069-7328-5

First published in the U.K. in 1990 by Argus Books.
Published by arrangement with Argus Books.
This edition for sale in the United States, Canada,
and the Philippine Islands only.

Library of Congress Cataloging-in-Publication Data

Stevenson, Paul, 1955–
The American Civil War/Paul Stevenson.
    p.   cm.--(Wargaming in history)
        ISBN 0-8069-7328-5
United States--History--Civil War, 1861–1865--Campaigns--
Simulation Methods.   I. Title   II. Series.
E470.S85 1990   89-26229
973.7'3--dc20   CIP

Typeset by Photoprint, Torquay, Devon.
Printed and bound by LR Printing Services Ltd, Edward Way,
Burgess Hill, West Sussex, RH15 9UA, England.

CONTENTS

INTRODUCTION

The American Civil War has been a major interest of mine for the past twenty years. I still discover new aspects of it every day, such is the wealth of material and documentation available. As an amateur historian, I realise that I will never sate my thirst for knowledge and understanding of this major event in American history, as new facts and opinions surface each year. One of the biggest literary efforts in recent times on the American Civil War has been the release of Time Life Books series *The Civil War* which is readily obtainable in this country and which contains many unpublished and useful snippets of information on uniforms and flags in particular, many of which are in colour. Furthermore, membership of The Confederate Historical Society, which publishes a quarterly journal, has greatly widened my studies into uniforms and flags. I can wholeheartedly recommend this organisation to any serious student of the Civil War.

As a wargamer, I have never been satisfied with any particular set of rules for this period and I suspect I am not alone in this. Indeed, most wargamers pursue the unobtainable perfect set of rules and, after many years in the hobby, one realises that they do not exist. Similarly, one should never be satisfied with one's own attempts at rule writing – the mental challenge of developing a set of rules is surely one of the most appealing, if at times frustrating, aspects of the hobby. In point of fact, no one set of rules can cover every facet of wargaming the Civil War. For example, we may wish to play skirmish games with 25mm figures, we may wish to play division level games with 15mm figures and corps level actions with 6mm figures. Indeed, we may not wish to use figures for our games at all. Board games offer other alternatives. In this spirit, I have not included any rules for wargaming but have provided plenty of ideas and background information for the wargamer to, if not write his own rules, at least analyse and criticise the rules he does use.

Finally, if you are looking for a general history of the war or an analysis of its causes and effects, don't look here. This is not what the book is about. Which is not to say that I subscribe to the view that wargaming is about gaming first and history second. In fact, one complements the other in building a more complete understanding of the period. I must therefore postulate that the reader has a general familiarity with history of the war, its main events and characters.

Paul D Stevenson
1989

1 ORGANISATION

INFANTRY

Regular Regiments consisted of from 2 to 4 battalions. Battalions usually served separately but sometimes in twos. More often, *ad hoc* battalions were formed from several companies within the regiment. Battalions were theoretically commanded by majors but, in practice, a senior captain usually commanded. Each battalion had 8 companies. Volunteer regiments consisted of 10 companies. Independent battalions were also formed of between 3 to 6 companies.

Regimental Headquarters Staff
Colonel
Lieutenant Colonel
Major
Lieutenant Adjutant
Lieutenant Surgeon
Assistant Surgeon
Hospital Steward
Lieutenant Quartermaster
Quartermaster Sergeant
Commissary Sergeant
Sergeant Major
2 Principal Musicians
24 Bandsmen (appointed at brigade level after 1861)

Company Organisation
Captain
First Lieutenant
Second Lieutenant (also 3rd Lieutenant in Confederate Army)
First Sergeant
4 Sergeants
8 Corporals
2 Musicians
82 Privates
Each company was split into 4 platoons and each platoon into 2 sections.

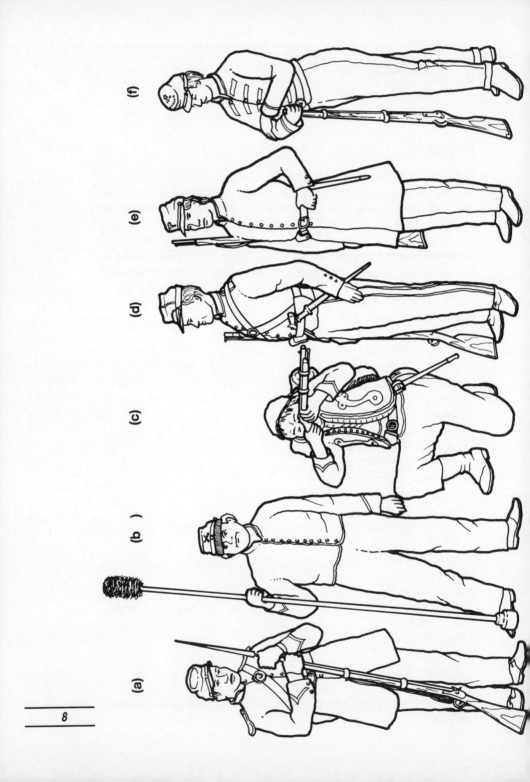

UNIFORM DETAILS

(a) **Private, United States Coloured Troops, 1864.**
Dark blue – Kepi and frockcoat; Sky blue – pants; Brass – Shoulder scales; Black – Straps and equipment; White – Gloves.

(b) **Cannoneer, United States Artillery, 1862.**
Dark blue – Kepi and shell jacket; Sky blue – Pants; Red – Jacket piping and pants stripe.

(c) **Private, 140th New York Infantry, 1864.**
Dark blue – Zouave jacket, vest, sash and fez tassel; Red – Fez, jacket trim, sash binding; Sky blue – Pants; Yellow – Edging to fez; White – Button-up gaiters.

(d) **Private, 18th North Carolina Infantry, 1861/62.**
Grey – Kepi, shell jacket and pants; Black – Kepi band and piping, collar and shoulder strap piping and stripes on pants, waist belt and equipment pouches; White – Webbing cross belts.

(e) **Private, 3rd South Carolina Infantry, 1861/62.**
Grey – Kepi, frockcoat and pants.

(f) **Private, 1st Texas Infantry, 1861/62.**
Grey – Jacket and pants; Dark blue or grey – Kepi with silver unit designation and star; Black – Trim on jacket and pants.

At the beginning of the war, several militia regiments were built up to strength and served as complete fighting regiments. A few of these continued in service throughout the war, such as the 14th Brooklyn (84th New York). Some regiments aimed their recruitment at specific types of recruit, such as Ellsworth's Avengers (44th New York), which required volunteers to be unmarried, able-bodied, under 30 years of age, over 5 feet 8

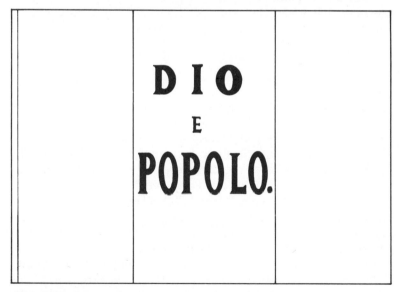

Flag of 39th New York Volunteers (Garibaldi Guards). Italian national colours with black lettering.

inches in height, of good moral character and of a high order of intelligence.

Artillery regiments were of 12 companies and heavy regiments serving as infantry in 1864 were very strong, around 1,200 men divided into 3 battalions.

Regimental Strengths In The Field

As there was no stringent medical examination, many unfit recruits actually joined up. The rigours of service soon weeded out poor physical specimens but illness, detached duties and battlefield casualties reduced regiments considerably. Apart from Wisconsin, the United States operated a policy of recruiting new regiments (to obtain political favours from newly appointed colonels). The Confederacy managed to top up some of the losses sustained by their regiments but numbers continued to dwindle throughout the war. Average strengths for Union regiments in 1861 were 700; 1862, 500; 1863, 320; 1864, 400; 1865, 500. Confederate regiments averaged 600 in 1861; in '62, 450; in '63, 350; in '64, 250 and in '65 only 150.

Confederate regiments throughout the army were similar in experience and numbers. New soldiers soon learned from experienced men in the regiment. In the Union army there was a greater diversity of regimental experience and strength. Sherman reckoned that it took fully one year to make a raw regiment an effective unit.

CAVALRY

The basic unit of tactical manoeuvre in a cavalry regiment was the squadron, and later, in the Union army, the battalion. In 1861, volunteer regiments and regulars were composed of 5 squadrons of 2 companies each. Each company was divided into 2 platoons. When the 3rd Regiment of United States Regulars was formed in May 1861 with 12 companies, a new sub-unit was introduced – the battalion – of which there were 3. This arrangement accommodated the new tactical thinking which called for support to the attacking sub-unit and a reserve to counter-charge. In July 1861, all Union regiments adopted a 12 company organisation – 6 squadrons – 2 per battalion. Confederate regiments retained the 10 company organisation.

Regimental Headquarters Staff
Colonel
Lieutenant Colonel
3 Majors (Union army only)
Major (Confederate army)
Lieutenant Adjutant
Lieutenant Quartermaster
Lieutenant Commissary
Lieutenant Surgeon
Assistant Surgeon
2 Hospital Stewards
Sergeant Major
Quartermaster Sergeant
Commissary Sergeant
Saddler Sergeant
Chief Farrier or Blacksmith

Company Establishment
Captain
1st Lieutenant
2nd Lieutenant (plus 3rd Lieutenant in Confederate army)
Quartermaster Sergeant
Commissary Sergeant
Saddler Sergeant
5 Line Sergeants
8 Corporals
2 Teamsters
2 Farriers
Saddler
Waggoner
2 Musicians
60 to 80 Troopers

As strength dwindled in Union regiments, battalions replaced the role of squadrons. Typically, a regiment on campaign had 3 battalions, each of 160 to 180 troopers. At Gettysburg, Union regiments averaged 360 men and Confederate regiments, 280. By 1864, Union regiments were around 250 strong and Confederates, 200.

ARTILLERY

Union batteries and early Western Confederate batteries usually had 6 guns; other Confederate batteries and late war Union batteries had 4 guns. Most Confederate batteries up until 1864 had

2 rifles and 2 smoothbore pieces which often operated as independent sections. A section was 2 guns and was commanded by a lieutenant. Captains commanded batteries. Sergeants commanded platoons which consisted of the gun, its limber and caisson, 9 gunners and 6 drivers. Teams were normally of 6 horses but 4 was quite normal in late war Confederate teams pulling lighter pieces. A travelling forge and battery wagon containing tools and equipment was attached to each battery. A gun required 3 crew members to remain in action. Including officers, NCOs, gunners, drivers, buglers and blacksmiths, the battery had a theoretical strength of 155 men. However, establishments in reality fell below this. At Gettysburg, Union batteries averaged 105 men and Confederate batteries, 90.

HIGHER ORGANISATION

Usually from 2 to 6 regiments of infantry or cavalry formed a brigade. In 1861 mixed brigades of foot and mounted troops could serve together in a brigade but this was unusual and not seen after 1861 in the Eastern Theatre. In the early part of the war, especially in Confederate armies, batteries could be attached to brigades. From 1862, batteries were grouped into brigades of 3 in the Union armies or battalions of 4 in the Confederate. Batteries attached to cavalry divisions were horse artillery (Gunners were mounted).

Confederate Infantry await attack.

Brigades were commanded by Brigadier Generals (or Colonels in the Union). Confederate brigades most often were composed of regiments from the same state but the Union paid less attention to this, though there were some all state brigades like the 'Philadelphia' and 'Excelsior' brigades.

Usually 3 brigades made up a division in the Union armies, or 4 in the Confederates. Early war Confederate brigades were of variable size and could consist of up to 6 brigades. Divisions were commanded by Major Generals (or Brigadiers in the Union). 2 to 4 divisions composed a corps. Corps commanders were Lieutenant Generals in the Confederate army and Major Generals in the Union. Army commanders were full Generals in the Confederate army and Major Generals in the Union army. When U.S. Grant was appointed General in Chief of the Union Armies he was awarded the rank of Lieutenant General, the only soldier to hold this rank since Washington.

Average Percentage Troop Types Available to Civil War Armies

	Union Armies	Confederate Armies
Infantry	80%	70%
Cavalry	14%	20%
Artillery	6%	10%

WARGAMES ARMY ORGANISATION

The armies below typify mid-war organisation, equipment and morale. Figure to men ratio is approximately 20–25:1. One model gun represents two pieces.

Union Army
Division Commander: Brig. Gen.
1st Brigade: Brig. Gen.
4 × Regiments Veterans, each of 10 figures, 2 figs with BLR per unit, rest with MLR.
2 × Regiments Green, each of 25 figures, with 2nd Rate MLRs or SB muskets.

2nd Brigade: Col.
5 × Regiments Seasoned, each of 15 figures with MLRs.

3rd Brigade: Col.
4 × Regiments Experienced, each of 20 figures with MLRs.

Assigned Divisional Units.*
Battery of 3 Napoleons, Seasoned.
Battery of 3 3″ Rifles, Seasoned.
Squadron of Cavalry, Experienced, 4 figures each with BL Carbine, sword and revolver.

Assigned from Artillery Reserve.†
Battery of 2 20 pdr Parrotts or 3 10 pdr Parrots.

Assigned from Cavalry Corps.†
Regiment of Experienced Cavalry, 24 figures, each with BL Carbine, sabre and revolver.

*Represents ⅓ of corps artillery. Cavalry used as provost guard, HQ guard or ignored.
†These detachments are proportionate to actual full army to create a balanced force for wargaming.

Private, 21st Virginia Infantry, 1861/62.
Uniform details: Grey – Kepi, frockcoat and pants; Black – Kepi band, collar and shoulder trim and stripe on pants, cartridge box and cap pouch; White – Webbing belts. Armed with 1842 musket.

Colour Sergeant, 12th Virginia Infantry, 1864.
Uniform details: Grey – Jacket and pants; White – Gaiters; Dark grey or blue – Kepi; Gold – Kepi trim (unusual); Crimson – Sash; Sky blue – Chevrons.

Confederate Army

Division Commander: Maj. Gen.
1st Brigade: Brig. Gen.
4 × Regiments Veterans, each of 10 figures all with MLRs.

2nd Brigade: Brig. Gen.
3 × Regiments Seasoned, each of 15 figures all with MLRs.
1 × Regiment Experienced, 20 figures with MLRs.

3rd Brigade: Brig. Gen.
1 × Regiment Veterans, 10 figures 2 with BL rifles, 8 with MLRs.
3 × Regiments Seasoned, 15 figures each, with MLRs.

4th Brigade: Brig. Gen.
3 × Regiments Seasoned, 15 figures each, with MLRs.

Artillery Battalion
3 × Batteries, each of 1 3" Rifle and 1 12 pdr Napoleon. Seasoned.
1 × Battery, 2 10 pdr Parrotts.

Assigned from Cavalry Corps
2 × Regiments of Seasoned Cavalry, each of 15 figures, ML Carbine, sabre and revolver.
Or 2 × Regiments of Veteran Cavalry, each of 10 figures, MLC, sabre and revolver.

Totals of Figures Required for Armies

	Commanders	Infantry	Mounted Cavalry	Dismounted Cavalry	Guns	Gunners
Union Army	4	245	28	21	9	36
Confederate Army	5	205	20–30	15–24	8	32

Notes: (i) Extra figures based as skirmishers can be provided (20% of total figure strength) or else individual figures are mounted separately for skirmishers; (ii) A prone figure placed behind a unit can denote that the unit is lying down; (iii) Breastworks to cover the frontage of the artillery and one brigade of infantry should also be provided for the Union army.

ORGANISING WARGAMES UNITS

There are many manufacturers of ACW figures; some of them have very extensive and comprehensive ranges. Figures are available in all scales. It is not always possible to match figures from different manufacturers in the same unit or even army, despite the fact that they may be nominally of the same scale. Some can be incompatible. ACW units can be the most varied of wargames units by virtue of the sheer mix of figures possible. For example, headgear can be extremely variable – slouch hats, straw hats, Hardee hats, French style kepis, flat topped kepis, even bearheads – all are available in many manufacturers' ranges. Uniform coats can be fatigue blouses, frock coats, shell jackets, shirtsleeves, and so on. Equipment can also be variable with light order, blanket rolls and knapsacks. Figures advancing with guns levelled or at high port position can form one type of unit; another can be made up with loading and firing figures. Figures marching at the slope can form another unit. (Incidentally it is only recently that manufacturers have begun to release figures in the 'at the slope' position – most of the time soldiers carried and charged with *slope arms*, only levelling bayonets in the last few yards to contact.)

Confederate Infantry overrun a battery of 3-inch rifles. (*Photograph by Stephen Foulk*)

Painting ACW Armies
Basic ACW figures are probably the easiest of wargames models to paint. Some gamers have a tendency to over-elaborate and even fantasise on the various trimmings and facings, which were rarely worn anyway. At 15mm scale, such elaboration is probably superfluous, and if attempted must be done with restraint.

'The Iron Brigade'. (*Photograph by Stephen Foulk*)

The basic blue and grey colours of the uniforms paint in well over black undercoats. Shadows can be left in folds and other areas of darkness to create an image of extra depth. For Union blue coats and kepis, I use a basic mix of blue and black paint and dry brush with a lighter tone where the textured surfaces allow this; otherwise, on a smoother figure, I highlight the shoulders, tops of the arms and maybe the front of the coat opening. The trousers are painted with sky blue – I would not advise trying to mix this from blue and white as the resultant shade is not correct. A wash of mid-blue is given to the trousers to tone the sky blue down. After a few washes, the sky blue colour of the trousers in reality faded to a pea green colour, therefore I usually mix in a little green to the blue wash to get the right effect. Finally, a little white is mixed in with the basic sky blue/pea green shade and the legs dry brushed or highlighted.

Confederate uniforms were not as dishevelled as some writers would have us believe. Certainly during the Antietam campaign, Lee's army was particularly ragged and dirty. This is perhaps understandable when one considers that the army had fought two major campaigns that same year. Also at this time, the system of uniform supply in the Confederacy was not effective and whilst 'butternut' (usually a reddish or yellowish brown shade) was common in 1862, by 1864, most Confederates were indeed wearing grey uniforms. That shade of grey was variable. In the West, a lighter shade was normally more common than that in the east. In the Army of Northern Virginia, Longstreet's Corps was outfitted in blue grey uniforms which were imported from England. These were sometimes trimmed in branch of service colours: red for artillery, yellow for cavalry and sky blue for infantry.

Private, 11th New York Volunteers (Ellsworth's First Fire Zouaves). Red – Fez, overshirt; Black – Scarf, leather equipment; Dark blue – Pants, sash, fez tassel; Silver – New York Fire Department badge. *Note*: Several units adopted this 'philibuster' style in emulation of Garibaldi's Redshirts. The 39th New York wore red shirts and black scarves at Bull Run too.

Private, 14th New York State Militia, 1861–64. Dark blue – Jacket, kepi top and band; Red – Kepi sides, shoulder knots, jacket front and trim, pants and blanket roll; White – Gaiters, canteen sling; Black – Belts and equipment; Brass – Buttons, clasps, buckles.

In the Wilderness, Confederates wearing this dark uniform were shot at by their own men. During the Gettysburg campaign, eye witnesses commented upon how much better equipped and dressed was Lee's army than the year before. When painting Confederates in grey uniforms, don't just use a pure grey from the tin but add a little tan or sand colour. Generals and regimental officers uniforms were often a light blue/grey colour – obtainable by mixing sky blue and grey. Confederate infantry uniforms were more often trimmed with black braid than with sky blue. Kepis were popular at first and were in branch of service colours. However, grey/butternut was more usual.

By 1863, two thirds of the Confederate soldiery had substituted slouch hats for kepis. I paint black hats by dry brushing the basic black undercoat with greyish blue. Lighter colour slouch hats I paint a basic white, wash with light tan or grey so that the sweat band appears darker in shade, then dry brush white. Leather equipment is best painted in reddish brown or blue grey and shaded with black ink. Much of the Confederate leather equipment was left in natural colours, rather than dyed black. Union blankets, as strapped to the tops of knapsacks, were either grey or light tan. Confederate blankets were of similar colours, though many home-made or civilian blankets were also used. Blanket rolls worn around the body – ie slung over the left (usually) shoulder – were wrapped in a rubber poncho or ground sheet. Confederate haversacks were white with white straps. Union haversacks were black with black straps. Canteen slings were normally white in both armies and cloth covers on canteens were either tan, grey or sky blue.

Guns are best painted reddish brown and most, like the Springfield and 1842 Musket, had silver metal fittings. Enfields had brown barrels with brass fittings, Remmington's had blue barrels and brass fittings. Buttons, kepi fittings and badges were mostly brass, as were sword hilts, guards and bayonet scabbard tips. Artillery pieces had brass (actually bronze) barrels if smoothbore, and gun metal or black barrels if rifled. Carriages, caissons, limbers and wagons were 'olive green' in the Union army (ie really a shade more like yellow ochre) and grey blue in the Army of Northern Virginia.

2   FLAGS

UNION FLAGS

Union infantry regiments carried two colours, a regimental and a national. Both flags measured 6 feet on the hoist and 6½ feet on the fly. The regimental colour was usually blue but white was also common. The regular regimental flag featured the American eagle in brown with white head, clutching a branch of laurels in green or gold and a sheaf of arrows in the other (left) claw. Scrolls in red, sometimes trimmed gold with gold letters, were positioned above and below the eagle. An arc of two rows of gold or silver stars surmounted the top scroll. There were several variants of eagle. The staff was topped by a gilt eagle. Volunteer regiments often carried their state flag or/and a special regimental flag (see illustrations).

The National flag had a blue canton featuring at first 33 and, by 1863, 35 stars arranged most often vertically in several variations of star grouping. Horizontal and circular star arrangements were also common. Stars were either gold or silver. Stripes were red. Regimental designations were usually inscribed on the centre red stripe. Both national and regimental colours had yellow fringes. Cavalry flags were similar but measured 2 feet 3 inches on the hoist and 2 feet 5 inches on the fly. Each troop

Flag of 1st Maryland United States Volunteers. National colour.

carried its own swallow-tailed guidon which was 2 feet 3 inches on the hoist and 3 feet 5 inches on the fly. The top half of the flag was red, the lower half, white. White letters on the red half and red on the white half indicated the troop letter. After 1862, a guidon based on the stars and stripes was used. Artillery regimental flags were yellow with gold crossed cannon instead of the eagle. Each battery had its own guidon which was like that of the cavalry. All flag cords were blue and white.

Flag of 37th New York Volunteers. Field – Emerald green; Top scroll – Dark blue; Bottom scroll – Red; Scrolls' trims and letters – gold; Fringe, battle honours, harp, shamrocks and scroll beneath – Gold with black lettering.

Brigades, divisions and corps headquarters were also authorised to carry flags. McClellan formalised headquarters flags into a system in 1862. HQ flags were to be small, square and flown underneath the national flag on the same pole. 1st Corps had a red flag, 2nd was blue, 3rd red and blue vertically, 4th red over blue. Division flags were 5 feet on the hoist and 6 feet on the fly; red for the 1st Division, blue for the 2nd, red and blue vertically for the 3rd, red over blue for the 4th. Brigade flags were of similar size and were striped in various combinations of red, white and blue. In May 1863, a new arrangement of formation flags was introduced together with corps badges to be worn on the uniform headgear. Corps HQ flags were mostly swallow-tailed, 3 feet on the hoist and 6 feet on the fly. 1st Division flags were white with the corps symbol in red, 2nd Division were blue with the symbol in white and 3rd Division flags were white with blue corps symbols. Ambulance flags were plain yellow, 1 foot 3 inches on the hoist and 2 feet 6 inches on the fly. Hospital flags were also yellow and had a large black 'H' in the centre of the field; they were 5 feet on the hoist and 8 feet 3 inches on the fly.

By 1864, many leading Union generals had designed their own personal flags. Meade's HQ flag was a large purple swallow-tailed affair featuring a golden eagle inside a silver wreath of laurels. Sheridan adopted a red over white swallow-tailed guidon, with a white star on the red half and a red star on the white half directly below it. Custer had several guidons at different times. His most usual was red over blue, bearing crossed white sabres. The Cavalry Corps of the Army of the Potomac had an HQ flag that was 3 feet on the hoist and 6 feet on the fly in blue, swallow-tailed and with a large red 'C' placed over white crossed sabres. Division flags followed the infantry pattern, 4 feet 6 inches on the hoist and 6 feet on the fly. The 1st Division had red crossed sabres on a white field, the 2nd had white sabres on a blue field and the 3rd had blue crossed sabres on white.

Flag of 20th Massachusetts Volunteers. Field – White; Top scroll – Silver-black letters, edged gold; Bottom scroll – Red, silver letters, edged green; Cloud – Orange; Sunburst – Gold; Shield frame – Gold; Top swirls – Gold; Lower swirls – Green; Battle honours – Gold, shaded black.

CONFEDERATE FLAGS

Every Confederate army had its own design of battle flag. Some units carried state flags and flags of their own design as well. The 'Stars and Bars' was carried by many units in 1861 but its similarity to the Union's 'Stars and Stripes' resulted in its being replaced by a battle flag based on a St. George's, or more commonly a St. Andrew's cross. Some cavalry units retained the stars and bars in guidon form throughout the war. The 'Stainless Banner' introduced in 1863 was too much like a flag of surrender to be used as a battle flag (though the 32nd North Carolina carried it). Some units in the Army of Northern Virginia cut the 'Southern Cross' canton from the flag and used this as a battle flag. In the Army of Tennessee, Polk's Corps usually used blue battle flags with a red St. George's cross edged in white, bearing 11 white stars. These flags measured 28 inches on the hoist, and from 46 to 52 inches on the fly. They were carried into late 1863. Bragg's Corps carried red flags with a broad St. Andrew's cross in blue, edged white and with three white stars on each arm. The flag was bordered with broad pink or white bunting. These flags averaged 42 inches on the hoist and 72 inches on the fly. Van

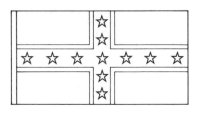

Polk's Corps battle flag, 1862/63.

Bragg's Corps battle flag, 1862/63.

Van Dorn's Corps battle flag, 1862/63.

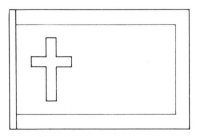

Missouri battle flag.

Dorn's Corps carried red battle flags with a white crescent in the top corner nearest the staff and 13 stars scattered across the field.

Most of these flags had a yellow and some a white border. These flags measured around 44 inches on the hoist and 60 inches on the fly. Missouri units carried a dark blue flag with a red border and a white Latin cross in the half of the field nearest the staff. These flags measured around 36 inches on the hoist and from 47 to 51 inches on the fly. In Hardee's Corps units carried blue flags with a white circle or elliptical disc and white border. Unit descriptions were frequently inscribed in the disc with battle honours on the border. Most of these flags measured around 30 inches on the hoist and from 37 to 42 inches on the fly.

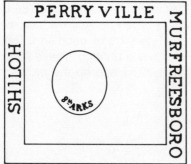

Hardee's Corps battle flag, 1862/63.

Johnston's battle flag, 1864/65.

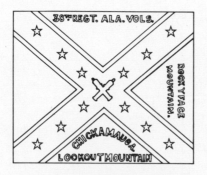

Polk's Corps battle flag, 1864/65.

Cleburne's Division battle flag, 1864/65.

When the Army of Tennessee passed into the hands of General J. E. Johnston at the end of 1863, that officer ordered a common battle flag to be carried by all units from early 1864. One flag was authorised per regiment. The flags were similar to those carried by the Army of Northern Virginia and displayed the 'Southern Cross'. They came in two basic sizes, 30 inches on the hoist by 39 inches on the fly for artillery and cavalry, and from 34 inches to 37 inches on the hoist by 51 to 54 inches on the fly for infantry. The flags were red with a blue St. Andrew's cross and edged white (this edging was generally broader than that of the Virginia army). The flags did not have borders. Cleburne's Division of Hardee's Corps did not accept the new flags and instead were issued with new blue flags of similar design to their original. Battle honours were applied in a more uniform way but some of the flags faded to a pea green colour due to poor dyes. These flags measured 30 to 32 inches on the hoist and 36 to 38 inches on the fly.

From 1864, Polk's Corps carried flags measuring 42 to 48 inches on the hoist and 53 to 55 inches on the fly.These flags were red with a dark blue St. Andrew's cross edged in white with 3 stars on each arm – none at the intersection of the cross. Forrest's cavalry had similar flags only smaller ie 37 inches on the hoist by 47 inches on the fly. (Note: Confederate cavalry, apart from the early part of war, made little use of guidons.)

In the Army of Northern Virginia, battle flags were much more standardised. These measured 48 inches square for infantry and 30 inches square for cavalry. First issues of the battle flag were in November 1861. These silk flags were replaced by cotton bunting flags from early 1862 onwards, and an extra star was added to the intersection of the cross making 13 total. First and second issue bunting flags as well as the silk variants had orange borders. A third issue had a white border and some units of the army were given this as early as November 1862 (ie Early's Division). D. H. Hill's Division received third pattern flags in December 1862, inscribed with battle honours in yellow. Battle honours where applied were most usually in white, but some were in silver or gold. Different methods of applying unit identifications to the flags were used.

At first cloth strips in white, with dark lettering and numbers, were attached to the flag, often on or near the border but occasionally in the centre at the cross intersection or in one of the red quadrants. Sometimes the unit identification was painted

Flag of Black Horse Troop, 4th Virginia Cavalry. 38ins. × 31ins. Based on Virginia's State flag. Field – Blue; Centre – White; Standing figure – Blue and red, trimmed yellow; Fallen figure – Blue, trimmed yellow; Lettering – Gold on dark blue ribbons; Fringe – Gold.

Flag of South Carolina Militia, Infantry. 78ins. × 72ins. Field – Blue; Fringe – White; Scroll – Red, yellow lettering, edging and decoration; Cords and tassels – Blue and white.

directly onto the flag, as many flags were left unmarked. By late 1863, the system of flag distribution and marking had become so efficient that battle flags, complete with uniform unit abbreviations and stencilled battle honours, were issued to complete divisions at a time.

Headquarters flags were similar in both Eastern and Western Confederate armies. These consisted of 3 horizontal bars for corps HQ and 2 horizontal bars for division HQs. A system of red, white and blue colours was used to designate the different corps and divisions. These flags measured 15 inches square.

WARGAMES FLAGS

Commercial flags of variable quality are readily available in the 15 and 25mm scales although the variety is restricted outside of the more usual Stars and Stripes and Southern Cross. Most Civil War flags are quite easy to paint and, if done well, can look as good as commercially produced items. The best method of flag construction is to wrap a paper rectangle around a metal staff (piano or florists' wire). If the flag is quite long, it is a good idea

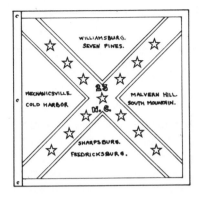

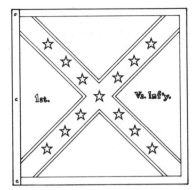

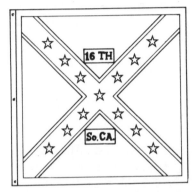

Army of Northern Virginia battle flags showing various methods of applying unit designations.

to cut the sides diagonally to create a hanging effect. Once painted, the flag can be bent into folds or even crumpled (a good method of hiding a botched paint job!). Flag cords can be made from cotton thread, knotted at each end and frayed out, then coated with glue to stiffen. Spear points can be simulated by daubing glue at the top of the staff and drawing it out when almost dry. Flag pole eagles pose a problem!

A variety of units can be created by having alternate command bases or flag figures. For example a Confederate unit wearing grey or brown uniforms could be said to be universal to any army or corps but their flag gives them away. Using a similarly painted command base but substituting a different flag, one can have a unit from a different army or corps. The same can be done with Union and Confederate flags. Many units on both sides wore both blue and grey at the start of the war – by having alternative command bases, one with a Union and the other with a Confederate flag, the wargamer can introduce some flexibility into his games, eg perhaps more Union regiments are required to meet a particular scenario.

3 TACTICS

INFANTRY TACTICS

Standard battle formation for an infantry regiment operating independently was six companies in line, two in reserve at 150 up to 300 yards in rear, and two companies skirmishing at a similar distance ahead. Skirmisher companies kept a proportion of their men as immediate supports to the skirmish screen at about 40 paces to the rear. Casey's *Infantry Tactics* of 1862 gave emphasis to the attack in column of divisions, ie with two companies abreast in double rank, four ranks deep with one company deployed as skirmishers and one company in reserve. Hardee outlined the particular functions of skirmishers in his *Tactics* thus:

'The interval between skirmishers depends on the extent of the ground to be covered but in general it is not proper that the groups of four men ('comrades in battle') should be removed more than 40 paces from each other. The habitual distance between men of the same group in open ground will be 5 paces; in no case will they lose sight of each other.'

Applying this to wargames terms, if we allow one pace per rank of a close order formation our skirmishers should cover a frontage four times greater. In other words, two wargames figures on skirmisher bases should screen eight close order figures. As most wargames rules allow a skirmish order figure two or three times the frontage of a close order figure, this clearly represents a thicker skirmish screen than was considered usual. Obviously, the more dispersed the skirmishers, the more difficult a target they present, but there will be a point where shooting at a target four paces from another will require a similar accuracy to shooting at targets dispersed over greater distances where windage is unlikely to cause incidental hits anyway. It is only at targets placed at less than four pace intervals that windage may achieve incidental casualties. Therefore, in a wargame we could take account of four types of formation ie close order, loose order, open order and extended order. To simplify our game we could base our figures to, say two main orders – close and open – and ignore the others.

Hardee laid down that any company in a regiment should

provide skirmishers but Casey's manual called for two companies of picked skirmishers in every regiment although this was not officially adopted. Certainly, some units did employ specific companies as skirmishers and equipped these with the best weapons available for the purpose. Whole units specially trained for skirmishing were raised on both sides. In 1864 Lee organised sharp-

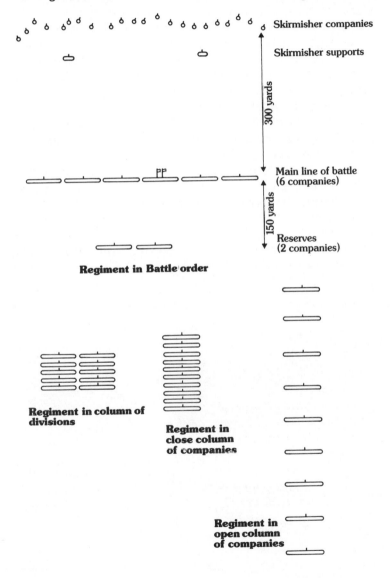

Skirmisher companies

Skirmisher supports

300 yards

Main line of battle (6 companies)

150 yards

Reserves (2 companies)

Regiment in Battle order

Regiment in column of divisions

Regiment in close column of companies

Regiment in open column of companies

shooter companies to serve with each brigade in the Army of Northern Virginia. Berdan's Sharpshooters are a well-known unit. They served in the East but the Western armies also had sharpshooter regiments such as the 14th Missouri. Major General Lew Wallace described their method of operation:

'A little before dawn, Birge's sharpshooters were astir. Theirs was a peculiar service. Each was a preferred marksman, and carried a long range Henry rifle with sights delicately arranged as for target practice. In action each was perfectly independent. They never manoeuvred as a corps. When the time came they were asked, "Canteens full? Biscuits for all day?" Their only order, "Alright; hunt your holes, boys." '

Some regiments were trained in the manner of the French Chasseurs to advance quickly in loose order to lessen casualties in an attack. They were trained to open fire at close range and then charge in with fixed bayonets. This was difficult to achieve as, once halted to fire, officers experienced problems in getting their men to move forward again. For this reason, attacks were often made with uncapped or even unloaded muskets. Lew Wallace's regiment, the 11th Indiana, were uniformed as zouaves and adopted the chasseur tactics. Several regiments in the Army of the Potomac received chasseur or zouave uniforms in recognition of their drill proficiency. Not all zouave regiments used chasseur tactics.

Brigade assault by Union Infantry on Rebel-held farmstead. (*Photograph by Stevie Willis*)

Columns were frequently used where mass at a point of weakness was needed. Regiments either deployed their companies one behind another in 'close column' of companies or else deployed on a broader front with two companies abreast in what was known as a 'column of divisions'. Where lines of attack were used, eg at Fredricksburg, the regiments often lost their impetus and halted to fire. A column was much more manoeuverable and could be controlled by the officers far easier than a line. Its drawback was that it would sustain higher casualties but even this could be offset by its ability to move faster across a fire zone and the greater likelihood of it bringing about a more decisive result than a protracted and ultimately more costly firefight. Two other columns were also used. Firstly, an 'open column' of companies, with the companies spaced out one behind the other with enough of an interval between to allow individual companies to wheel into line at right angles to the direction of march. Secondly, 'column of route' which was two, or more often four, files deep. Both types of column were used to bring a battle line quickly into position.

Higher Formation Tactics

Above regimental level there were as many tactical formations in use employed by brigade, division and corps commanders.

Tactics were flexible and strongly influenced by the French school. The usual formation for a brigade operating as part of a corps, was to deploy its regiments in successive lines, one behind another, with space enough between each regiment to wheel to a flank. Regiments were often closed up if the brigade was in reserve. On most battlefields of the Civil War, troops were often deployed in dense masses. When brigades operated as part of a division, they would often by deployed with their regiments in line abreast, with perhaps one or two brigades in line and the remainder deployed with their regiments in close column in reserve.

A few examples illustrate the wide variety of higher tactical formations. At 2nd Fredricksburg in 1863, Newton's Federal Division used the French 'ordre mixte' in its assault on Marye's Heights. One of its brigades was deployed with three regiments in line and with one regiment deployed as skirmishers from each brigade in front. On either flank of the line was a further brigade deployed in regimental column of divisions. This formation succeeded where successive lines had failed in the first Battle of Fredricksburg. Here, attacking waves tended to stop short of the Rebel positions and return fire. Exposed in the open and shooting at well-covered troops, it was a firefight they could not win. The

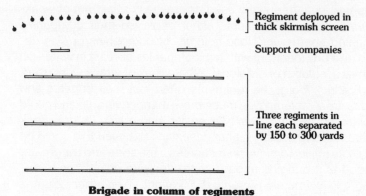

Regiment deployed in
thick skirmish screen

Support companies

Three regiments in
line each separated
by 150 to 300 yards

Brigade in column of regiments

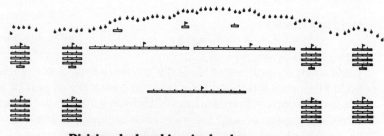

Division deployed in mixed order
NB. Three brigades each of four regiments. Flank brigades
with regiments in column by divisions. Centre brigade
with three regiments in line and one skirmishing.

usual attack formation for a brigade was to form it into a column
of regiments with the first regiment supplying the skirmishers.
Upton's Federal brigade attacked in this fashion at Spotsylvania.
Only the first line had capped rifles.

Their job was to charge into the enemy breastworks and clear
the line from left to right. The second wave had to occupy the
trenches in preparation for a counter-attack from the enemy's
second line. The third and fourth waves had to lay down just short
of the works in reserve. The whole attack was properly planned
and co-ordinated and the attackers gained a lodgement in the
enemy's works. Unfortunately, the supporting attack by Mott's
Division of tired veterans broke up under artillery fire before it had
got fairly started. Upton lost 1,000 men from his brigade and

returned with 300 prisoners. One of the biggest columns of attack seen in the war was sent in two days later to emulate Upton's success on a grander scale. Barlow's whole division was formed into a column fifty files deep. The leading regiment was deployed in a dense skirmish screen with one or two pace intervals between each man, only thirty yards ahead of the main column. Moving through the dark and damp woods it approached the Confederate 'Mule Shoe' fieldorks at a quick step for a few hundred yards. Over the last 500 yards, the column went in over the enemy works at the double quick, taking the Rebels off guard and capturing hundreds of prisoners. At Kennesaw Mountain in 1864, Newton's Union Division was formed in a column almost as dense as Barlow's, ie in column of regiments formed by column of divisions. For his attack at the Petersburg 'Crater', Burnside organised his formations thus:

> 'My plan would be to explode the mine just before daylight in the morning or at about 5 o'clock in the afternoon; mass the two brigades of the coloured division in rear of my first line, in columns of division – double columns closed in mass – the head of each brigade resting on the front line . . .'

The plan called for the leading regiments to sweep left and right down the enemy's penetrated line with the reserves following through to the enemy's second line. The plan might have worked, only Grant stood down the coloured troops on political grounds.

The Union 'Irish Brigade'. (*Photograph by Stevie Willis*)

These troops had drilled for several weeks and were in good condition. Unfortunately, veteran white troops without the necessary assault training were substituted and the attack was a disastrous failure.

When 'Stonewall' Jackson arranged his corps for the crushing flank attack at Chancellorsville, he allowed 150 yards between each division which deployed in line of brigades with their regiments in column. At Chickamauga, Hindman's Confederate Division was formed with its brigades in column, 200 yards between each. Such compact formations facilitated some control in these woodland battles, but at Shiloh the Confederate Army deployed in successive waves of corps. This insane formation was responsible for the breakdown of command during the battle and necessitated an impromptu rearrangement of the command structure, leading to inevitable delays and unco-ordinated attacks. Learning from this experience, the Confederate General Bragg deployed his second line 800 yards behind the first at Stones' River to avoid co-mingling of his units. Once units got mixed up it was difficult for their officers to maintain control.

The battle could bog down into a protracted firefight or panic could easily grip such disorganised masses. For similar reasons the passing of reserves through a fatigued front line could also be dangerous and might lead to confusion. This was called a 'passage of lines' – the flank companies of the front line units were moved behind the main front line while reserves passed through the gaps thus created in column. Where the front line was not particularly thick, a reserve line was sometimes advanced through it – the front line was told to lie down as the reserves went over their line. To illustrate this tactic (and to underline further the unwillingness of veterans in the attack), Bruce Catton writes of Birney's first attack at Petersburg on 18th June 1864 thus:

'His principal column was formed in four lines, with veteran troops in the first two lines and oversized heavy artillery regiments, untried but full of enthusiasm, in the last two. The men were lying down when the order to charge the rebel works came in, and as the officers shouted and waved their swords the inexperienced artillerists sprang to their feet while the veterans ahead of them continued to lie prone. The veterans looked back, saw the rookies preparing to charge, and called out: "Lie down, you damned fools, you can't take them forts!"

'One of the artillery regiments, 1st Massachusetts heavies, accepted this advice, lay down again, and made no charge. The other one, 1st Maine, valiantly stayed on its feet, ran forward through the rows of prostrate men and made for the Confederate line.'

A similar incident was recorded at Gettysburg. As Barnes Division retreated from the Wheatfield during the fighting on the second day, Zook's Brigade found themselves barred by these units. Zook then shouted, 'If you can't get out of the way, lie down and we will march over you!' Zook's men did indeed march over them and charged into the Wheatfield – Zook, riding at their head, was the first to fall.

Confederate Infantry charge – note casualties. (*Photograph by Stevie Willis*)

CAVALRY TACTICS

The main tactical manual used by both sides throughout the Civil War was the 'Poinsett Tactics' of 1841. These were based entirely on the current French system and called for a two rank deployment. In 1862, Colonel Philip St. George Cooke's tactics were officially adopted but only superseded Poinsett in the Western armies. General Wheeler's manual for the Confederate cavalry was similar to Cooke's and advocated a single rank deployment. According to theory, it took two years to train a cavalryman. As nearly everyone thought that the war would be 'over by Christmas' it was therefore not surprising that the government discouraged the formation of volunteer cavalry regiments.

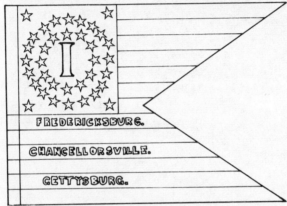

Flag of I Troop Guidon, 6th Pennsylvania Cavalry. National colours, gold stars, troop letter and battle honours (latter outlined in black).

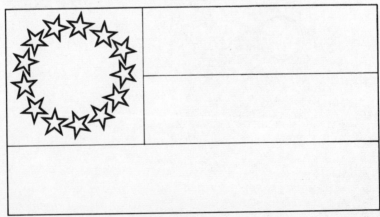

Flag of 1st Maryland Confederate Cavalry, 1863. National colours, silver stars.

Column of fours was the usual marching column and the regiment would normally approach the battle zone in such a formation, deploying perhaps off a road, into column of platoons. Each squadron would then form line and move into close column of squadrons if the ground permitted. This formation was frequently employed for shock action. Battalions with squadrons abreast could also be used in the attack, again where space permitted. The first battalion was placed in front and served as the main attacking force, the second battalion was kept within wheeling distance for close support, and the third acted as reserve some distance behind the supports. Rarely were the squadrons of a regiment deployed in line, as the distance covered by such an extended formation made control difficult. A squadron deployed on a frontage of 50 to 66 yards. Cavalry manoeuvred at various speeds but a good average walk/trot speed for mounted troops would be 150 yards per minute – a canter and gallop/charge would cover about 300 to 400 yards in a minute.

For dismounted action, one man in four was delegated as a horse holder. If the mounts were secured, this could be stretched to one man in eight, which is what General Wilson did at Selma. Horse holders galloped unridden horses to the rear. The regiment would be deployed as a thick line of skirmishers or a single, loose order line, perhaps with a couple of skirmish companies thrown out 300 yards ahead. Often on each flank, one or two companies were retained as mounted supports, especially when engaged against enemy cavalry.

ARTILLERY TACTICS

Artillery personnel were the most professionally expert soldiers in either army. This was due to the technical demands of their branch of service. In action, the gun crews and drivers were reliable and steadfast, partly because they attracted a better class of recruit but also because they were thoroughly trained. The presence of artillery was a great morale boost to raw troops. At first, batteries were attached to infantry brigades but, as the armies grew larger, the need for greater control led to the grouping of batteries into brigades or battalions.

Normally, guns were deployed 14 yards apart. Each piece occupied 2 yards, giving a six-gun battery a frontage of 82 yards and a four-gun battery a frontage of 50 yards. Limbers, and caissons behind them, were parked in the rear of each gun and required a depth of 50 yards. Drivers and horse teams faced towards the enemy positions for psychological as well as practical reasons. Batteries attempted to take up position on the reverse slopes of gently rising ground in order to deflect enemy missiles and if such a position was not available, the earth in front of the battery would be thrown up a couple of feet high. A battery carried about 100 rounds of ammunition per gun, of which three-quarters was solid shot and shrapnel, and the balance shell and canister.

At Gettysburg, the Union artillery had over 220 rounds for each of its guns; the Rebels had about 180 rounds per gun. In action, a battery could shoot off all its ammunition in one hour, the crews being capable of firing two rounds per minute. Batteries out of ammunition would be withdrawn to replenish at the trains in the rear. After an hour's shooting, however, the gunners would be fatigued. The Union commander, Hunt, complained that the Union artillery was firing off all its ammunition as quickly as it could – 3 rounds per minute in order to get out of the firing line. Hunt ordered that one round per minute was the optimum for accuracy and conservation of ammunition. A trained crew could unlimber and fire a round in 30 seconds and could limber up again in less than a minute. A battery required three times longer than a single gun. Guns could also be slowly withdrawn by 'prolonges', long ropes fixed to gun and limber to give withdrawing fire.

24 pdr smooth bore siege gun in battery protected by pallisades. (*Photograph by Stevie Willis*).

4   WEAPONRY

ARTILLERY

Types of Artillery

There were two kinds of artillery regiments – heavy and light. Each regiment was composed of 12 batteries. These did not serve together on campaign however (see Chapter 1). Heavy artillerymen served guns over 20 pounder as a rule, though some light batteries were equipped with 20 pdrs, and some heavy artillery batteries substituted lighter guns. Of light artillery, there were two tactical organisations – field artillery, where the gunners walked, or rode on the ammunition chests of limbers and caissons if doubling into action; and horse artillery, where all the gunners were mounted on horses. Of heavy artillery, there was siege and garrison/seacoast artillery. The heaviest siege artillery taken into the field was of 30 pounder but no more than a handful were used in most battles by any one side. McClellan, in particular, favoured siege artillery and expected to make use of it at Williamsburg and Richmond. Although some 30 pounders were used at Malvern Hill, siege guns proved a 'white elephant' in the Peninsula.

Also included in the siege artillery train were mortars – usually 8 and 10 inch. A 13 inch mortar, named 'Dictator', was used during the siege of Petersburg and moved by railroad flat-car. Mountain artillery saw some use, normally in East Tennessee and West Virginia, but one or two batteries were to be found in the main armies in Virginia and on the Mississippi. Mountain artillery in transit was pack carried on mules and assembled for action. Towards the end of the war, when trench warfare became the norm, a good deal of use was made of Coehorn mortars. They were first used at Cold Harbour in 1864. F/2nd Battalion, 15th New York Heavy Artillery had 8 × 24 pdr brass Coehorns. They fired at a fixed angle of 45° and had a maximum range of 1,200 yards – range was adjusted by reducing the charge. After the Wilderness battles, it became clear that flat trajectory guns would not be of much use in the wooded regions and would be ineffective against troops in trenches, so Grant broke up his artillery reserve and reduced his field batteries to 4 instead of 6 guns.

Comparison of Civil War Artillery

Artillerists were divided into two schools of thought regarding the merits of rifled bore or smoothbore guns. Rifles were very accurate, could outrange smoothbores and could fire a heavier shell. The 10 pounder Parrott, for example, was of a similar weight and calibre to a 6 pounder smoothbore, yet had a 26% longer range and fired a shell 55% heavier. On the other hand, a smoothbore could deliver a heavier charge of canister. A rifle round could jam if not loaded carefully – heavy Parrott rifles also had a habit of exploding.

At Fredricksburg, the two 30 pounders employed by the Confederates burst, one after 38 rounds and the other after 53. Even the 20 pounders could explode, so brittle were their cast iron barrels. Hunt, the Army of the Potomac's chief of artillery, started a campaign to rid the army of these weapons after Antietam but did not purge them completely until after May 1864. As a rule, the regulars preferred the 12 pounder Napoleon smoothbore for its reasonable range, accuracy and ability to discharge heavy rounds of canister. Preferred weapon of the Union Horse Artillery was the 3 inch rifle because of its lightness and accuracy. The Confederates used a few imported English Whitworth and Armstrong breech loaders which were used in a muzzle-loading role. They were extremely accurate and had a range of four miles. McClellan also had four in his reserve.

32 pdr smoothbore Barbette. (*Photograph by Stevie Willis*)

Artillery Projectiles

There were four main types of ammunition. Smoothbores fired spherical ammunition with fixed charges for speed of loading and rifles fired cylindro-conoidal ammunition (which looked similar to modern artillery shells).

Canister. Canister was simply a can of light tin which contained a number of cast iron shot about the size of a golf ball. A canister round for a Napoleon contained 27 balls. Three such rounds could be fired in a minute by a trained crew out to a maximum range of 400 yards. Double and treble rounds of canister could be loaded ranging out to 250 and 100 yards respectively. In firing such heavy loads, guns lighter than Napoleons could be thrown completely over by the recoil. Rifled field artillery fired rounds containing around 18 balls. After Gettysburg, canister rounds of 78 marble-sized balls were introduced which were lethal at close range but lacked the ballistic effect of heavy canister.

Shell. Sometimes called common or explosive shell. This type of projectile was a light hollow cast sphere for smoothbores or a cylindro-conoidal casing for rifles. Smoothbores used time-fused shells, while rifled shells detonated either by time-fuse or on impact. When a shell exploded it would tear into about seven large chunks. Confederate shells were particularly ineffective with only 1 in 15 actually bursting. Spherical shells had better incendiary effects than rifled artillery shells.

Shot. Solid shot was used by both rifled and smoothbore artillery. Rifled shot tended to bury itself in the ground and was mainly used for battering, in which role it was more effective than roundshot but lacked the ballistic effect of roundshot, which increased the potential range of smoothbore artillery. Shot was used against dense targets but was less effective than shell (even if the shell did not explode it could still cause damage), against most other targets.

Shrapnel. So called after its British inventor, Henry Shrapnel, and also referred to as 'spherical case' shot when fired by smoothbores. This projectile was a hollow cast iron round filled with musket balls (78 for a Napoleon), which, if fired correctly, burst overhead and just in front of its target. This was quite tricky to achieve if the target was opening or closing the range. Fuses for Napoleons were cut to explode at ranges of between 500 to

1,500 yards. Generally speaking, shells could be ranged up to 25% less than the maximum range obtainable when firing solid shot. Case shot could also be fired to explode within a few feet of the muzzle of the gun spraying balls up to 200 yards or so, and was frequently used in emergencies when the supply of canister had been exhausted. Shrapnel was an anti-personnel round which more often wounded than killed in comparison to other projectiles.

Field Artillery Statistics

Type	Bore ins.	Weight lbs.	Round	Charge lbs.	Range yards
12 pdr Howitzer 1841	4.62	788	8.9	0.75	1072
24 pdr Howitzer 1841	5.82	1318	18.4	2.00	1322
6 pdr Smoothbore Gun 1857	3.67	884	6.1	1.25	1523
12 pdr Napoleon Smoothbore 1857	4.62	1227	12.3	2.50	1680
3″ Ordnance (Rodman) Rifle 1861	3.00	820	9.5	1.00	2788
10 pdr Parrott Rifle 1861	3.00	890	9.5	1.00	2970
12 pdr James Rifle 1857	3.67	875	12.0	0.75	1700
12 pdr Blakely BL Rifle	3.10	700	12.0	1.50	1760
12 pdr Whitworth BL Rifle	2.75	1100	12.0	1.75	8800
20 pdr Parrott Rifle 1861	3.67	1750	20.0	2.00	4400

Composition of Batteries

At the start of the war, battery make-up in terms of weapon types was often variable, even on the Union side. At Bull Run, for example, Battery E, 2nd U.S., had 2 × 12 pdr James rifles, 2 × 6 pdr smoothbores and 2 × 12 pdr howitzers. On the Confederate side, the Washington Artillery of New Orleans had 6 × 6 pdr smoothbores, 4 × 12 pdr howitzers and 3 × 6 pdr rifles. Chew's Confederate horse artillery battery in 1862 had 1 × Blakely Rifle, 1 × 3 inch Ordnance Rifle and 1 × 12 pdr howitzer. At Cedar Mountain, Pegram's battery had 2 × Napoleons and 2 × 3 inch rifles. The Army of the Potomac managed to field batteries of a uniform type of gun by 1862 but, in other Union armies, batteries

Stuart's Horse Artillery.

could vary in composition as widely as the Confederates. Quite often it was a question of supply. Everyone wanted Napoleons and 3 inch rifles but it took a few years for the Confederate armies and the Western Union armies to standardise most of their armament.

Artillery Representation in the Civil War Armies

	Weapon	Percentage in Union Army	Percentage in Confed. Army
First Bull Run, 1861	6 pdr SBs	6	70
	12 pdr Howitzers	10	20
	12 pdr Napoleons	15	0
	6–12 pdr Rifles	41	10
	20 pdr Rifles	15	0
	30 pdr Rifles	2	0
Antietam, 1862	6 pdr Smoothbores	1	58
	12 pdr Howitzers	1	3
	12 pdr Napoleons	42	10
	10–12 pdr Rifles	44	29
	20 pdr Rifles	8	0
	30 pdr Rifles	2	0

Gettysburg, 1863	6 pdr Smoothbores	0.3	0
	12 pdr Howitzers	0.5	9
	24 pdr Howitzers	1	0
	12 pdr Napoleons	39	38.7
	10–12 pdr Rifles	58	49
	12 pdr Whitworth Rifles	0.5	1
	20 pdr Rifles	1.6	3.5
	30 pdr Rifles	2.1	0
Wilderness, 1864	12 pdr Howitzers	0	5
	12 pdr Napoleons	44	48
	10–12 pdr Rifles	54	45
	20 pdr Rifles	2	3

These figures are for Eastern armies. Those in the West had a greater diversification of weaponry, which was comparatively inferior, also. For example, Rosecrans' Union army as late as 1863 was equipped as follows:

6 pounder smoothbores × 32
12 pounder howitzers × 24
12 pounder Napoleons × 8
20 pounder Parrotts × 2
10 pounder Parrotts × 34
3 inch Ordnance rifles × 4
James rifles × 21
12 pounder Wiard rifles × 2
6 pounder Wiards × 2

Types of American Civil War fences.

Even a cursory glance over the figures reveals that the Napoleon was not used to the extent that is popularly imagined and that rifled guns were predominant. Neither is it true that the Confederate artillery was mostly Napoleons; in fact McClellan's field artillery in the Seven Days' battles was 45% Napoleons, and the Confederates had none at all.

Type of American Civil War fence.

Proportion of Artillery in Civil War Armies

Battle	U.S.A.	C.S.A.
1st Bull Run	1 gun per 700 men	1 gun per 660 men
Shiloh, 1862	1:400	1:370
Antietam, 1862	1:230	1:140
Chancellorsville, 1863	1:350	1:280
Gettysburg, 1863	1:230	1:260
Chickamauga, 1863	1:320	1:360
Spotsylvania, 1864	1:330	1:250
Atlanta, 1864	1:390	1:520
Nashville, 1864	1:320	1:240

SMALL ARMS EFFECT ON THE BATTLEFIELD

Most firefights between infantry took place at ranges less than the quoted 500 yards effective range of muzzle-loading rifles. Paddy Griffith in his book *Rally Once Again* discusses this subject at some length, and proves conclusively that firefight ranges were little more than those of Napoleonic times in the early war period, and only slightly more than this in the late period. Paddy reckons that the average range for firefights in the West was 100 yards and, in the East, 136 yards. This was perhaps attributable to the poorer weapons employed out West and the more generally wooded terrain. My own reading substantiates Paddy's findings but one incident is perhaps worth citing of a long range firefight at First Bull Run, recorded by the artist Frank Vizetelly of the *Illustrated London News*:

> 'This is the only case in which I saw two regiments positively engage each other and these did no more than blaze away at each other at a distance of three hundred yards until both were badly cut up. The Alabama regiment especially suffered, and when they retired, they left the ground covered with their dead and wounded. The 71st (New York) lost heavily; but behaved exceedingly well, loading and firing as if on parade. I think that if the bayonet had been used more freely the matter would have been sooner decided, and with less loss of life. On the hill at the back a Confederate battery was playing on the 71st. I was on the right of the latter regiment.'

The 71st New York was a well drilled Militia regiment known as the 'American Guard'. The Alabama regiment was probably the 4th, and the battery no doubt was Imboden's firing from the Henry Hill. The incident is revealing in that it shows how a unit armed with rifles beat another with a majority of smoothbores.

Apart from the Western troops in Union service, it was normally the Confederates who got the better of their opponents in a firefight. Stonewall Jackson recognised the fighting qualities of the Westerners he encountered in the 'Valley' when he wrote:

> 'As Shields' division is composed principally of Western troops, who are familiar with the use of arms, we must calculate on hard fighting to oust Banks.'

Livermore provides some interesting statistics which give an indication of the effectiveness of sharpshooters in the Civil War, viz. a company of 64 skirmishers lying prone, firing 6 rounds per minute at another line deployed at 3 feet intervals and firing back at them at a range of 500 yards, will cause 0.45 casualties per minute. If the shooters were standing, this would reduce their effectiveness by 20%. Recruits fired at 50% less effect than veterans. If the target was skirmishers spaced at 5 yard intervals, then the shooters would be likely to achieve only half the stated number of hits. Finally, carbines at 500 yards were 40% less effective than rifles. With muzzle-loaders, the rate of fire would be one third less than the breech-loaders quoted and, if shooting prone, would at best manage one shot every minute, giving 0.075 casualties per minute. Using Livermore's figures, we can estimate that a regiment of 640 soldiers would score 1.2 hits using muzzle-loaders, standing firing at a prone target at 500 yards, over one minute. If the target was standing, and we assume that the shooters would be 50% more effective, we come up with a figure of 2.4 hits at 500 yards. (Such low hit probabilities are also given in Paddy Griffiths' *Battle*, p. 39.)

Private, 5th New York Duryea's Zouaves.

It is difficult to assess the effect of small arms in firefights. Rarely are there recorded statistics applicable to any one shoot-out between two opposing units over a set period of time at any one range. Rather, we have a multiplicity of factors to consider in determining just what sort of effect small arms had on the battlefield. Two examples of firefights, taken from Gettysburg, illustrate the low hit probability of Civil War firefights, even at close ranges. Baxter's Union brigade of 1,300 men inflicted 600 casualties on O'Neal's attacking brigade and routed it (O'Neal had 1,688 men). Rodes, who commanded the division to which O'Neal belonged, reported, 'The whole brigade was repulsed quickly and with loss.' Thus in a very short time – probably 5 minutes or so – Baxter's brigade had shot about half their strength of the attacking Confederates at a range of perhaps 100 yards. Then, turning against Iverson's attacking brigade, they shot down 450 Confederates at a range of 80 yards, apparently with one volley, then counter-charged and captured 400 of them. In both cases, Baxter's men had fired from behind a stone wall. Against O'Neal, Baxter's men had scored 0.461 casualties with one round per man, though possibly two, ie a minute's fire. Against Iverson, Baxter inflicted 0.346 in a minute's fire (allowing for two rounds per man firing). Noticeably the second fire was less effective than the first, which may indicate the greater effectiveness of the first volley.

Confederate line of battle.

During the fighting on the second day at Gettysburg, Barksdale's Mississippi Brigade of 1,600 men engaged 1,516 men of Graham's Union brigade at a range of 200 yards. Barksdale's men caused 570 casualties in a few minutes, say five total, giving 0.071 hits per minute of fire per man. When the fighting was very close, the damage inflicted could be appalling. On the first day at Gettysburg the 24th Michigan engaged the 26th North Carolina at a range of 20 paces. After an exchange of volleys, the Carolinans charged and drove back the Michiganders. The 24th Michigan went into action with 496 men and lost 397 – 80% loss. The 26th North Carolina with 800 men lost 549. It is clear, here, that the more experienced Union regiment inflicted greater damage on the Confederate attackers but was broken by weight of numbers.

Firefight at Antietam

In studying these statistics it must be remembered that the fighting at Antietam was particularly bloody. Nevertheless, a close study of the movements and positions of the units engaged during the fighting between 6.00 and 6.45 am of 17th September, 1862, reveals that the Confederates were more effective in combat than the Union troops.

Union Brigades Involved	Strength	Killed and Wounded	Missing	Percentage Loss
Hartsuff	1200	579	20	50
Duryea	1800	292	35	15
Christian	800	225	29	30
Seymour	1200	155	0	15
Phelps	425	100*	0	25
Total	5425	1351	84	27

*Allows 54 casualties inflicted by Hood's attack after 6.45 am.

Confederate Brigades				
Hays	550	334	2	60
Lawton	1150	546	21	50
Trimble	700	229	6	30
Total	2400	1109	29	47

5,400 Union troops shot 1,100 Confederates in 45 minutes.
120 Union troops shot 2.5 Confederates in 1 minute.
Union troops scored an average 0.204 hits per man in 45 minutes.

2,400 Confederate troops shot 1,300 Federals in 45 minutes.
53 Confederate troops shot 3 Federals in 1 minute.
Confederate troops scored an average 0.524 hits per man in 45 minutes.

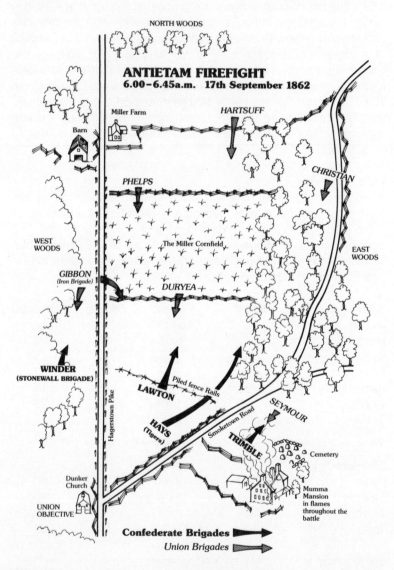

ANTIETAM FIREFIGHT
6.00–6.45a.m.   17th September 1862

NORTH WOODS

Miller Farm

Barn

HARTSUFF

CHRISTIAN

PHELPS

WEST WOODS

The Miller Cornfield

EAST WOODS

GIBBON
(Iron Brigade)

DURYEA

WINDER
(STONEWALL BRIGADE)

LAWTON

Piled fence Rails

SEYMOUR

HAYS
(Tigers)

Smoketown Road

TRIMBLE

Cemetery

Hagerstown Pike

Dunker Church

UNION OBJECTIVE

Mumma Mansion in flames throughout the battle

Confederate Brigades ➤
Union Brigades ⇒

Note: Although the Union was on the overall offensive, during this phase of the fighting the Confederates attacked and counter-attacked every thrust made by the Union troops. Most of the fighting was at ranges well under 100 yards, and in open ground.

Comparison of Civil War Small Arms

Firearm	1.	2.	3.	4.	5.	6.
1822 Flintlock Musket	.69	50	100	200	8″ @ 50	2
1842 Percussion Musket	.69	50	150	300	8″ @ 50	2–3
1842 Musket Converted to Rifle	.69	100	300	600		2–3
1841 Harpers Ferry Rifle (Converted)	.58	150	300	700	6″ @ 50	2
1855 Harpers Ferry Rifled Musket	.58	200	400	1000	8″ @ 100	2–3
1861/63 Spring- field Rifled Musket	.58	250	500	1300	6″ @ 100	2–3
1862 Remington Rifle	.58	350	600	1500	4″ @ 100	2–3
1853 Enfield Rifled Musket	.577	250	500	1100	6″ @ 100	2–3
1854 Lorenz Rifled Musket	.54	250	500	1300	8″ @ 100	2–3
Whitworth & Kerr (Long Range Rifles)	.45	600	1200	1800	6″ @ 500	1
1859/63 Sharps Breech-loading Rifle	.52	450	700	1500	5″ @ 100	6–8
NB. Berdan's Sharpshooters					5″ @ 200	
1860 Henry Repeating Rifle	.44	400	600	1500	5″ @ 100	15
1863 Spencer Repeating Rifle	.56	400	600	1500	5″ @ 100	10–12
1856 Colt Revolving Rifle	.56	250	500	1000		5–6
1855 Enfield Carbine	.577	200	400	800	6″ @ 100	2–3
1859/63 Sharps Carbine	.52	300	500	800	5″ @ 100	6–8
1863 Spencer Carbine	.56	200	400	1000	6″ @ 100	10–12

1856 Burnside

| Carbine | .54 | 150 | 300 | 600 | 5″ @ 100 | 6–8 |

Gallager, Smith, Starr, Joslyn and Maynard Carbines as Burnside.

Hand guns and

| revolvers | .36 or .44 | 10 | 25 | 100 | | |

| Shotguns | 12 gauge | 25 | 50 | 100 | 12 buck- shot per barrel | |

KEY
1. Calibre
2. Battle Range ie the extreme range at which attackers are likely to be stopped in their advance by fire from an equal number of defenders.
3. Effective Range ie the extreme range at which shots are likely to be effective.
4. Maximum Range ie the greatest distance to which a weapon is sighted.
5. Accuracy. A group of hits placed within a specified number of inches from the bull's eye at a given range.
6. Rounds per minute under ideal circumstances.

Proportion of Types of Infantry Weapons in Civil War Armies

What follows is a general and, in some cases, subjective look at the types of armament available to Union and Confederate armies at different periods throughout the war. Nevertheless, enough data has been compiled to give the wargamer a fair idea of how to 'equip' his miniature troops.

Percentage of Weapons Used in Eastern Theatre

Weapon	Army	1861–62	Late 1862	Mid 1863	1864–65
Flintlock Muskets	U.S.	–	–	–	–
	C.S.	10	–	–	–
Percussion Muskets	U.S.	30	12	7.5	–
	C.S.	25	20	3	–
2nd Rate Rifles	U.S.	33	25	15	–
	C.S.	45	29	15	8.5
1st Rate Rifles	U.S.	35	60	75	90
	C.S.	20	50	80	90
Breech-loaders	U.S.	1.5	3	3	5
	C.S.	–	1	1.5	1.5
Repeaters	U.S.	–	–	–	2
	C.S.	–	–	–	–

Western Theatre

Flintlock Muskets	U.S.	9.5	–	–	–
	C.S.	25	10	–	–
Percussion Muskets	U.S.	40	30	22.5	5
	C.S.	50	45	35	15
2nd Rate Rifles	U.S.	30	25	20	10
	C.S.	20	30	20	29.4
1st Rate Rifles	U.S.	20	43.5	55	80
	C.S.	5	15	45	55
Breech-loaders	U.S.	0.5	1	2	3.5
	C.S.	–	–	0.5	0.5
Repeaters	U.S.	–	.25	.5	1.5
	C.S.	–	–	.1	.1

It should be noted here that in 1861–62 many Confederates were armed with squirrel rifles, shotguns and bowie knives only. The 44th Mississippi had to arm its rear rank men with sticks, such was the shortage of weaponry. Before the Peninsula Campaign in Virginia, several regiments of Whiting's division had a score of unarmed troops in the ranks. Tennessee troops suffered particularly from shortages – only 20% of their troops could be armed by the spring of 1862. The 20th Regiment considered itself fortunate to have its members armed with 1812 Tower Muskets!

The variety of armament within any one unit could be a quartermaster's nightmare. Of the total number of Confederate regiments at Bull Run, a third are known to have had a mixture of smoothbore and rifled muskets. Take the case of the 1st Virginia – Company K had 1841 rifles, F and H had 1855 rifles and the remaining companies had 1822 and 1842 muskets. Even as late as Gettysburg and on the Union side, some regiments had a miscellany of weaponry.

Normal practice throughout the war was for regiments to arm their flank, or skirmisher, companies with the better weaponry available to the unit. Thus, regiments armed with smoothbores might have at least one company armed with rifles. Smoothbores with flintlocks could be rendered useless by foul weather. At Mill Springs, the Confederates, armed almost wholly with such weapons, lost the battle due to the ineffectiveness of their guns in the drizzle. Percussion locks used caps instead of loose powder to contain the ignition charge. These were either rolls of caps in the early guns (Maynard system) or separate copper caps which fitted onto the nipple of the lock in later systems. Both types increased the rate of fire possible with a muzzle-loading weapon (but not significantly) in the hands of the average soldier. Firing a charge of buck and ball ammunition at very close range, a smoothbore could be very effective as demonstrated by the 12th New Jersey at Gettysburg. Opportunities for such close-in fighting as this were limited however and the rifle was the preferred arm.

Many of the 1842 muskets were converted to rifles. Few breech-loaders saw service, though some units had a company or two armed with the weapon. The Sharps breech-loader found favour with Berdan's United States Sharpshooters but not with the 11th New York Fire Zouaves – eight companies were armed with 1859 Sharps and two companies with muzzle-loading Enfields. The regiment went on strike until it received the favoured arm, the Enfield, which they maintained was the most suitable gun for zouaves! As for repeaters, these weapons saw even more limited use, although a surprisingly high number of soldiers bought their own guns, usually either a Henry or a Spencer. Spencers were not available until mid-1863. Colonel Wilder armed his mounted infantry brigade with Spencers purchased with his own funds. The brigade fought a successful action at Hoover's Gap and defeated a Confederate force twice its strength. By the end of '63, Spencer carbines became available and some infantry, as well as most of the Union cavalry, were equipped with this weapon. General Wilson, commanding a Cavalry corps in the West wrote of the repeaters:

> 'Green regiments, that you could not have driven into a fight with the old arms, became invincible the very moment that good arms were placed in their hands.'

CAVALRY SMALL ARMS

At first the Union cavalry was barely armed at all. The regulars had the old single-shot horse pistols but many volunteer units had only the sabre and perhaps one in ten men were armed with a carbine. By mid-1863, however, the Army of the Potomac's cavalry was equipped with breech-loading carbines of some description. A year later, most of the volunteer regiments had the Spencer but the regulars clung on to their Sharps. In the West, the Union cavalry was described by Wilson as 'a museum on horseback.' When he took command of it in the autumn of 1864, Wilson armed his troopers with Spencers. His 10,000 troopers played a major role in the defeat of Hood at Nashville. The following year, Wilson brought Forrest to heel in Alabama.

Confederate cavalry preferred shotguns and pistols to sabres but, as the war went on, their style of fighting changed to more dismounted action. A reliable carbine was needed. The Enfield carbine and shortened versions of the rifle variant became standard armament by 1864. Some Confederate cavalry regiments were entirely armed with the Sharp's carbine, for example the 1st Virginia and the 1st Mississippi. The Confederates could not manufacture the metallic cartridges required by repeaters.

MACHINE GUNS

The machine gun made its debut on the battlefields of the Civil War. There were three main types of hand-cranked machine guns and two multi-barrelled volley guns, all of which saw very limited use in the war.

The Agar, or Union Repeating Gun, was a light two-wheeler with a galloper carriage, complete with a bullet-proof shield. It was known as the 'Coffee Mill Gun' because of the shape of its ammunition feed hopper situated over the breech. Rate of fire was 100 rpm. Two guns saw action with the 28th Pennsylvania Volunteers and proved effective by shooting up two squadrons of Rebel cavalry at 800 yards near Middleburg, Virginia, on 29th March, 1862. After this they were not seen again in the field as, for some reason, they were considered 'unreliable and unsafe to operate'. Despite this, a war correspondent reported them in use with the Union army at Chattanooga in 1863.

The Gatling Gun was a superior weapon and capable of 200 rpm. Also, it was less likely to overheat. Several Union generals ordered these guns, and paid for them privately. In 1864, Butler and Hancock each had a dozen Gatlings.

The Confederates had their own machine gun, the Williams, which had a maximum range of 2,000 yards. The gun was loaded by hand with paper cartridges, each containing two 1 pounder roundshot. It was capable of firing 60 rounds per minute. The ammunition used was designed to ricochet, hence the increased range of the Williams gun (the Union weapons ranged to 1,200 yards). The trouble was that the Williams had a barrel of low grade steel which, after 10 minutes of sustained fire, swelled so much that it had to be allowed to cool for half an hour. Despite this, the Williams saw extensive use. Seven, 6-gun batteries were assembled and attached to infantry brigades. Schoolfield's battery fought with Pickett's Brigade at Seven Pines in 1862. Giltner's

Texas brigade also employed a battery at Blue Springs on 10th October 1863.

The volley guns were hardly innovative but are included here for completeness. The Billinghurst Requa Battery Gun had 25 barrels which discharged simultaneously a clip of .25 cal. bullets. Seven volleys could be fired in a minute and maximum range was 1,000 yards. The weapon became virtually useless in damp weather and was often employed to defend covered bridges or in fieldworks. The Vandenburg Volley Gun had from 85 to 451 barrels enclosed in a single thick tube. It was a very heavy and unmanageable weapon with a vicious recoil. It was never used in the field.

Flag of 20th New York State Militia. Field – White; Scrolls – Blue with gold lettering and trim; Coat of arms – Gold, shaded brown; Fringe – Gold.

SHOOTING – WARGAMING POINTS
Small Arms
1. Effective ranges for rifles under 450 yards, carbines under 350 yards, smoothbore muskets under 100 yards.
2. Restricted visibility of troops firing whilst prone, unless firing from gentle slope.
3. Increased difficulty of obtaining hits when firing up or down steep hills.

4. Decreasing danger zones with range.
5. Morale value of holding fire.
6. Detrimental morale effect on troops receiving a first concerted enemy volley.
7. Rapid fall off in effectiveness of fire subsequent to first volley.
8. Closer the range, the more likely troops are to stand in open under fire to deliver rapid return fire.
9. Troops in cover less likely to respond to enemy fire unless directly attacked.
10. Ability of troops with breech-loaders to move whilst firing and loading.
11. Difficulties of loading muzzle-loading rifles prone.
12. Greater effectiveness of skirmisher fire with breech-loaders.
13. Recognition of two grades of rifled muzzle-loaders.

Artillery
1. Greater chance of hitting with rifled guns.
2. Greater hitting power of rifled guns eg in counter battery or demolition.
3. Devastating effect of smoothbore canister on close order targets.
4. Unreliability of Confederate shells.
5. Greater incendiary effect of smoothbore shell.
6. Vulnerability of gun crews to skirmishers where a return of fire is less effective.
7. Visibility restrictions over 1,000 yards.
8. Effectiveness of mortars – ineffectiveness of other artillery against trenches.

5 COMBAT

BATTLE STATISTICS

Armies involving over 20,000 men on both sides are listed and thus represent the biggest battles of the war.

Eastern Theatre

Year	Name of Battle	Confederate Strength	Losses	Union Strength	Losses
1861	1st Bull Run	32,000	1,982	35,000	2,896
1862	Seven Pines	26,000	6,134	26,000	5,031
	Gaines' Mill	54,000	8,300	36,000	6,837
	Malvern Hill	56,000	5,355	35,000	3,214
	2nd Bull Run	54,000	9,474	63,000	14,462
	Antietam	45,000	11,172	87,000	12,410
	1st Fredricksburg	78,000	5,377	116,683	12,653
1863	Chancellorsville	60,000	12,463	130,000	17,287
	Gettysburg	77,500	28,000	93,500	25,000
1864	Wilderness	61,000	8,000	118,000	17,666
	Spotsylvania	50,000	10,000	100,000	18,399
	Drewry's Bluff	25,000	3,000	35,000	4,500
	North Anna	40,000	900	25,000	1,973
	Cold Harbour	58,000	1,500	110,000	7,000
Army Average		51,000	7,976 (15.6%)	74,000	10,666 (14.4%)

Western Theatre

Year	Name	Confederate Strength	Losses	Union Strength	Losses
1862	Fort Donelson	20,000	15,000	22,000	2,640
	Shiloh	40,000	10,694	51,000	13,047
	Corinth	22,000	4,800	23,000	2,500
	Stones River	37,700	10,266	43,400	13,249
1863	Champion's Hill	23,000	3,850	37,000	2,440
	Chickamauga	66,000	18,454	57,000	16,170
	Chattanooga	33,000	7,000	56,000	5,824
1864	Resaca	67,000	2,600	109,000	3,500
	Kennesaw Mountain	60,000	442	100,000	1,200

Peach Tree Creek	25,000	3,000	28,000	1,700
Atlanta	25,000	8,000	25,000	3,720
Jonesboro	24,000	2,000	55,000	1,500
Franklin	29,000	6,250	23,000	2,320
Nashville	38,000	9,000	55,000	3,600
Army Average	36,357	6,554 (18%)	46,100	5,244 (11%)

Bloodiest Battles of the War in Terms of Percentage Losses

Name of Battle	Overall Percentage Loss	Confederate Loss	Union Loss	Winner
Stones River	28.5%	27%	30%	Union
Chickamauga	28%	28%	28%	Confed.
Ocean Pond	27%	20%	34%	Confed.
Gettysburg	26.5%	28%	25%	Union
Shiloh	25%	25%	25%	Union
Atlanta	23.5%	32%	15%	Union
Antietam	21%	28%	14%	Union
Perryville	21%	22%	20%	Union
2nd Bull Run	20.5%	18%	23%	Confed.

INFANTRY VERSUS INFANTRY

Morale

The majority of the fighting took place between lines of infantry sometimes standing fully exposed, but more often kneeling and shooting prone from whatever cover was available. It was awk-

140th New York Infantry.

ward to load a muzzle-loading musket from a recumbent posture, hence rates of fire were low and firefights were prolonged when both sides settled down to an exchange of shots. A determined bayonet charge could often decide matters but Civil War officers experienced great difficulty in getting their men to charge in such situations.

In the Civil War, panic was endemic among the early volunteers. At the First Battle of Bull Run, the entire Union army fled at a turn of their fortunes. At Shiloh, much of Grant's army ran from the battlefield and cowered beneath the bluffs at Pittsburg Landing, taking no part in the battle that day. As the war went on, the soldiers grew less likely to panic, although they remained volatile throughout, exhibiting great daring and recklessness on one hand and the potential to be easily alarmed on the other. By way of illustration, the reputation of the Confederate 'Stonewall Brigade' is well known, yet the whole brigade fled from a flank attack delivered by one third of its numbers at Cedar Run in 1862.

Civil War regiments were especially wary of their flanks, particularly in woods where the numbers of the enemy were uncertain and the fear of isolation very real. Yet many commanders were less than circumspect about the protection of their formation's flanks. At Antietam, Sedgewick, who was a fairly good commander, marched his entire division in close column of brigades into the West Wood thinking he would penetrate the Rebel position, only to be charged in flank by a fresh enemy division. Sedgewick's corps commander, Sumner, could offer no solution to the 'bad fix' in which his men were placed and merely shouted, 'Back boys, for God's sake move back!' In twenty minutes the Union division suffered a loss of 2,210 men out of 5,000. Units moving to the rear could also cause a panic, especially if troops were under pressure. At Antietam's 'Bloody Lane' one of Gordon's Alabama units changed front to the flank and rear to meet a flanking attack when the whole brigade saw this as an order to retire, then fled.

The average Civil War veteran was a pragmatic combatant. He would only continue to fight if he felt there was an even chance of winning. The Union General Schofield remarked, 'The American soldier fights very much as he has been accustomed to work his farm or run his sawmill: he wants to see a fair prospect that it is going to pay.' In writing about the Confederate soldier D. H. Hill commented, 'He knew when a movement was false and a position untenable and he was too little of a machine to give in such cases the whole-hearted service which might have redeemed the blunder.' In formulating wargames rules, we must bear in mind the volatile nature of the Civil War soldier. Morale scores should be widely variable, especially so for inexperienced troops. The best way to represent this might be to throw a 12-sided die for the morale of green troops and two normal 6-sided dice for experienced troops. Morale factors for veterans should be weighted more heavily if things are going well or badly. For example, if scores for morale fall below a certain number, a further morale reduction should be made to the score.

Conversely, if morale situation factors are favourable, and above a set number, then additional factors could be added. However, veterans are less likely to panic or become over-enthusiastic, and so their behaviour as a result of a morale check should be modified. Regular troops are much the same as veteran citizen soldiers, only more reliable and more likely to fight on in a tight spot. On the other hand, regulars are less likely to become too enthusiastic as General Wood noted: 'The regulars are too sharp. They know when they are whipped but the volunteers don't; they will fight as long as they can pull a trigger.'

Flag of 5th New York Duryea's Zouaves, 1862.

Of course, Wood's comments presuppose that the volunteers are well-trained. For example, at Gaines' Mill the 5th New York Zouaves lost nearly half their numbers and yet dressed ranks under fire before advancing again. Similarly, at Groveton the Iron Brigade stood for hours exchanging volleys with veteran Con-

Flag of 11th New York Volunteers (Ellsworth's 1st Fire Zouaves).
68ins. × 54ins. Field – White; Centre – Painted fireman's equipment with wreath of roses; Large lettering – Gold, shaded red; Ribbon – Grey, edged gold with gold lettering shaded black; Leading edge – Gold; Fringe – Red, white and blue.

federates in its first battle and lost one third of its strength. Equally, raw recruits could be seized with a sudden panic if they had received little training – for example, the 11th New York Zouaves routed after they had been charged by cavalry and had witnessed the demise of one of their supporting batteries at First Bull Run. Thus it can be demonstrated that raw troops were not necessarily poor troops unless they had been little trained. Conversely, veteran troops could frequently perform badly. Mott's Division, in advancing to the support of a Union break-through at Spotsylvania in 1864, quickly ran back to some woods in their rear when they came under artillery fire. Clearly, the once proud division was no longer fit for combat, and was broken up. In our wargames we need to recognise the effect not just of experience but also of training on morale.

For example units can be classed according to experience as:
Greenhorn – completely without battle experience.
Experienced – having seen 'the elephant' (ie combat).
Seasoned – having reached the peak of combat efficiency through several combat experiences.

Veteran – very experienced and battle-wise troops who are unlikely to take risks.

'Old Lag' status – veteran troops who have been fought out and suffer battle fatigue.

Units can also be classed according to training:

Untrained – incapable of performing any but the simplest tactical manoeuvres and likely to fall into disarray under battlefield conditions. Applicable to the early war units.

Trained – moderately well-drilled units which may contain a mixture of veteran and green soldiers.

Well-trained – seasoned troops and veterans who will be well-trained by virtue of experience, also including inexperienced units which may have reached a high standard of drill.

Flag of 1st Regiment Cherokee Mounted Rifles.
79ins. × 45½ins. Based on 1st National Flag. Centre – Red stars indicate the five civilised Indian tribes; Lettering and cords – Red.

Flag of Choctaw Nation.
Field – Blue; Centre – Red; Ring and weapons – White.

Infantry Combat Performance

It was not until late in the war that practice with live ammunition became usual. At First Bull Run, many units went into action with less than three weeks training. Following the fiasco there, generals made sure that their armies were ready before embarking on a new campaign, much to the annoyance of politicians and populace. In the West, at Shiloh, the troops were perhaps better drilled and consequently the battle was far bloodier. Looking at the Antietam casualty statistics, it becomes obvious that the more experienced Confederates were twice as good with their firearms as the Federals. Also, during this battle the Confederate lines were spread thin in places when compared with those of their enemies. Very often, too, raw troops received substandard firearms which decreased their effectiveness. Again, raw troops tended to fire too early and at long range. This, of course, had a negligible effect on an attacking unit, who would continue to advance. With their guns emptied the raw troops would often not reload to try another volley but would run.

Even commanders of veteran troops realised the morale effect of having a loaded weapon in the face of an enemy attack. Confederate General Gordon commented that 'troops with empty guns' could not have withstood the attack made by the Federals at Antietam. Seasoned troops, however, sometimes opened fire too early or not when so ordered. According to Lt. Colonel Rice, the Union infantry at Gettysburg along the whole line started an irregular and hesitant fire as Pickett's charge swept up towards their positions, and then increased to rapid file firing. Even when troops managed to fire a second volley, this would be hurried and misdirected. This, of course, would hearten the attackers who, seeing the unsteadiness in the defenders' ranks, would be willing to press their attack. In the face of a determined bayonet charge all but the best troops broke. At this point, many prisoners would be taken – the attackers having won the morale battle by their determination to close. Once a regiment broke, the panic could infect neighbouring units. Veterans would more often fall back to regroup, but raw troops invariably went out of control and ran for the rear. General Law recalled the attack of his brigade at Gaines' Mill:

'The Confederates were within 10 paces when the Federals broke cover, and leaving their log breastworks, swarmed up the hill in rear, carrying the second line with them in their rout.'

At Gettysburg things were a little different – the Union troops were the seasoned 5th Corps – as J. Hoke explains:

United States Coloured Troops.

'the enemy (Confederates) came on yelling and running with the fixed bayonet charge which so few troops can withstand; but the patriots did not waver . . . it was a mêlée, a carnival of death.'

After Pickett's charge had managed to penetrate the Federal line on Cemetery Ridge, with only 150 men, Webb, the brigade commander on the spot, experienced considerable difficulty getting his men to counter-attack following the rout of the 71st Pennsylvania from the wall it had defended. The 72nd Regiment, in reserve, stopped the Confederates with a volley but refused to charge. On their left, the two reserve regiments of Hall's brigade were not so timid:

'The two lines came together with a shock which stops them both and causes a slight rebound. Foot to foot, body to body and man to man they struggled, pushed, strived and killed.' (A Massachussetts soldier.)

At such close quarters, units could not remain on the firing line for long. Typically twenty minutes was about all a unit could stand in close-range combat. Troops would load and fire as fast as they could. At two rounds per minute and forty rounds per man, a unit could not continue for longer. The Louisiana Brigade of Hays lost more than half its men in less than twenty minutes in an open field during which time it had exhausted its ammunition. At Second Bull Run, Starke's Louisiana Brigade did continue the action after it had run out of ammunition by throwing stones from the railroad cut which they defended. An alternative to this was to order a bayonet charge but most troops saw lack of ammunition as a good excuse to go to the rear.

Nevertheless, despite some hesitancy by his men, the colonel of the 20th Maine got his soldiers to charge down a hillside and rout the attackers of his position on Little Round Top at Gettysburg. As the war progressed such self sacrifice was less evident, especially on the Union side.

Flag of 51st New York Volunteers.
Field – Dark blue; Upper scroll – Red; Lower scroll – Grey; Lettering, borders to scrolls and frame to coat of arms – Gold; Coat of arms – Sky blue; Left-hand figure – Red/white; Right-hand figure – Cream/black.

Woodland Fighting
As large parts of the average Civil War battlefield was covered with trees, it became important that the commanders learned how best to operate in such terrain. In stacking up waves of attacking troops, commanders frequently had their plans thwarted by the resultant confusion that occurred when the front line was stopped or delayed by enemy action or terrain, causing a pile-up of successive lines. Even without such occurrences, woods acted like a filter to attacking troops. Where control was loose, troops entering a wood might not even

emerge on the other side, preferring the cover afforded by the trees to an open field. Fighting in woods was a nerve-wracking business. Although the soldiers had cover, they met the enemy at deadly range due to limitations of visibility. Troops in woods were never fully convinced of support being there to their flanks and could get extremely anxious about this.

It frequently happened that enemy troops blundered into each other in woods at very close range – sometimes striking an exposed flank as has already been noted. Commanders had to adopt means of controlling their forces in woods. Barlow's attack at Spotsylvania in 1864 was guided by compass. In the Wilderness, Grant made extensive use of field telegraphs, assigning a wire-laying mule to each of his brigades. Despite all the difficulties, the soldiers soon had woods fighting down to a fine art. General Harris, Army of Northern Virginia, explained the techniques used:

'When a regiment or a brigade advanced through a heavily wooded country such as the Wilderness, the point of direction was established, and the officers instructed to conform to the movements of the 'guide' company or regiment. Each regiment, moreover, was provided with a right and left 'general guide', men selected for their special aptitudes, being good judges of distance, and noted for their steadiness and skill in maintaining the direction.

'Then again, the line of battle was greatly aided in maintaining the direction by the fire of the skirmishers, and frequently the line would be formed with a flank resting on a trail or woods road, ravine or watercourse, the flank regiment in such cases acting as the guide. In advancing through thick woods the skirmish line was almost invariably strengthened, and while the 'line of battle' covered by the skirmishers, advanced in two deep line, bodies in the rear usually marched in columns of fours, prepared to come by a 'forward into line' to the point where their assistance might be desired. I never saw the compass used in woods fighting.

'Practical experience taught us that no movement should be permitted until every officer was acquainted with the object in view and had received his instructions. I may add that brigade and regimental commanders were most particular to secure their flanks and to keep contact with other troops by means of patrols.'

The implications of Harris' comments can be applied to the table top by handicapping the morale of units without visible flank supports in woods, by slowing the movement – perhaps drastically – of troops not in column of route in a wood, and by incorporating random movement off to the left or right of a unit's intended line of advance if it does not have a flank resting on a linear obstacle during its movement through a wood. Units without skirmishers in front should be surprised if they encounter enemy troops in a wood.

Brigade Action

As many wargames are fought on a divisional and brigade level, it might be as well to look closely at how a brigade actually fought as part of a division. I have focused on Kershaw's Confederate brigade in action at the Peach Orchard, Gettysburg on July 2nd. Kershaw's Brigade was part of McLaws' Division and belonged to Longstreet's Corps which, with the exception of Pickett's Division, was poised to strike the Union left from the Peach Orchard to the Devil's Den. My description is largely based on Kershaw's own account of the fighting, which is interesting in that we learn how orders were transmitted, how movements can go

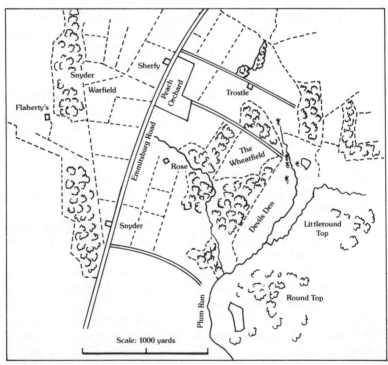

'Brigade action'. Map showing terrain over which Kershaw's brigade operated.

wrong, and how individual units act and react in combat. Kershaw's Brigade was composed of the following units; the 2nd, 3rd, 7th, 8th and 15th South Carolina Regiments and the 3rd South Carolina Battalion; total 2,200 men. Losses – k, 115; w, 483; m, 32 = 630 (28.6%).

Kershaw had been ordered to attack the Union positions at the Peach Orchard by Longstreet. Following a countermarch, Kershaw got his brigade into position behind the stone wall which runs from Flaherty's on his left to Snyder's on his right. 'This was done under cover of my skirmishers, who engaged those of the enemy near the Emmitsburg road.' On inspection of the Federal positions, Kershaw realised that, if he attempted to carry out Longstreet's order, he would expose his right to a flank attack from the Wheatfield area. Having communicated this information to McLaws, the latter deployed his division with Semmes Brigade 200 yards in rear of Kershaw, Barksdale's Brigade on Kershaw's left and Wooford's in rear of Barksdale's. Cabell's battalion of artillery was posted on Kershaw's right along the stone wall with one of Kershaw's regiments – the 15th South Carolina – in support of their right flank. Meanwhile, Hood's division moved around to the right and commenced its attack up the Emmitsburg Road, as per Lee's orders, and at almost right angles to McLaws' division. Kershaw was ordered to link with Hood's advance by swinging around towards the Peach Orchard, and told that Semmes would follow in his rear while Wooford advanced in support of Barksdale on his left. 'These instructions I received in sundry messages from General Longstreet and General McLaws, and in part in personal communication with them.' (Kershaw). At 5.30 that afternoon the attack went in.

'I received the order to move, at a signal from Cabell's artillery. They were to fire for some minutes, then pause, and then fire three guns in rapid succession. At this, I was to move without further orders. I communicated these instructions to the commanders of each of the regiments in my command, directing them to convoy them to the company officers. They were told at the signal to order the men to leap the wall without further orders, and to align the troops in front of it. Accordingly at the signal, the men leaped over the wall and were promptly aligned; the word was given, and the brigade moved off at the word, with great steadiness and precision, followed by Semmes with equal promptness. General Longstreet accompanied me in this advance on foot, as far as the Emmitsburg road. All the field and staff officers were dismounted on account of the many obstacles in the way.'

Upon reaching the road, and almost halfway to his objective, Kershaw heard Barksdale's drums beating the assembly and knew then that he was unsupported. [Apparently Longstreet intended this attack in echelon from the right, starting with Hood's division – obviously Kershaw was unaware of his overall plan.] The left wing of Kershaw's brigade composed of the 2nd and 8th Regiments and the 3rd Battalion passed the left of Rose's buildings and charged for the battery in the Peach Orchard. The 3rd and 7th Regiments advanced eastwards into the woods before the 'Wheatfield' and towards a stony hill nearby. The attack on the Peach Orchard was going well and it appeared that the cannoneers were about to desert their guns when the order came to 'move by the right flank,' by some unauthorised person. Returning to their guns, the Federals opened a destructive fire of canister. 'Hundreds of the bravest men of Carolina fell, victims of this fatal blunder.' Meanwhile, in their advance to the wood,

'the 7th Regiment had lapped the 3rd a few paces, and when they reached the cover of the stony hill I halted the line at the edge of the wood for a moment, and ordered the 7th to move by the right flank to uncover the 3rd Regiment, which was promptly done. It was no doubt this movement, observed by someone from the left, that led to the terrible mistake which cost us dearly.'

Dismounted Union Cavalry.

The Federals then attacked Kershaw's position on the stony hill flanking his right which was soon supported by one of Semmes' regiments. Kershaw called in his 15th Regiment, which was to the right and rear of Semmes some 2 to 3 hundred yards away, and his 2nd Regiment to his left, while the 3rd and 7th Regiments exchanged volleys with the Federals at 200 yards range. Reinforced by a further two brigades, the Federals again flanked Kershaw's right.

'The 7th Regiment finally gave way, and I directed Colonel Aiken to re-form it at the stone wall about Rose's. I passed to the 3rd Regiment, then hotly engaged on the crest of the hill, and gradually swung back its right as the enemy made progress around that flank. Semmes' advanced regiment had given way. One of his regiments had mingled with the 3rd and amid rocks and trees, within a few feet of each other, these brave men, Confederates and Federals, maintained a desperate conflict . . . I feared the brave men around me would be surrounded by the large force of the enemy constantly increasing in numbers and all the while gradually enveloping us. In order to avoid such a catastrophe, I ordered a retreat to the buildings at Rose's.'

Noticeable here is the way in which formations were aligned on natural or man-made terrain features which acted as markers for deployment – once one unit was in position, others took station on the flanks or to the rear. In most wargames, we tend to ignore the effect of terrain and the importance of roads on the battlefield – or, at least, those roads that lead onto the battlefield, which were features along which commanders could order their units to advance to the desired position. Similarly, terrain features were used by which to reform a broken unit or re-dress ranks etc. Although Kershaw's advance was across open country, the alignment of his brigade still suffered disruption because of minor obstacles leading to the partial overlapping of two of his regiments.

This sort of thing happened on a larger scale during Pickett's famous charge the following day and on innumerable other occasions in Civil War battles. Not many wargames rules allow for the eventuality of units advancing at variable rates and moving off course. Often, the wargamer is free to regulate the speed of his advance, halt and dress ranks etc at a whim, when in fact this was difficult to co-ordinate, especially under fire, and would only be attempted by very well-drilled troops. Also of interest in Kershaw's account is the manner in which he received his orders, usually through his division commander but sometimes through his corps commander. Once he had arrived at his forming-up position, ie along the stone wall to the west of the Emmitsburg Road (see map), he refrained from carrying out Longstreet's original order but went through his division commander (standard military protocol) and advised that the Union position was too strong for a direct attack. Here we have a case where a commander has been allowed to use his discretion.

At Shiloh, although several of his brigade commanders pointed out that the 'Hornet's Nest' position was too strong to be attacked frontally, Bragg insisted that his original orders should be obeyed. Longstreet, in this case, was obviously more ready to listen, though he still got the timing of his attack wrong, allowing Kershaw to attack unsupported, and restraining Barksdale's successful charge on the Peach Orchard longer than was necessary. Indeed, it was Barksdale's and Wooford's attack that took the pressure off Kershaw and allowed him to rally his shattered brigade, with the assistance of Colonel Sorrel of Longstreet's staff. Longstreet himself directed operations about 500 yards in rear of the front line and appeared to have accompanied McLaws. Longstreet's commanders had all received their instructions at 4.00 pm that afternoon and, after some twenty minutes bombardment, Hood's division advanced. (Incidentally Hood, in direct contravention of orders, moved towards the Devil's Den in order to flank the Union left, instead of attacking directly up the Emmitsburg road – a classic case of a capable subordinate changing his orders to suit the situation.)

Inexplicably Kershaw did not get the signal to advance until one and a half hours later, receiving no support until 6.30 pm when Barksdale was allowed to charge. Clearly, Longstreet was keeping to a schedule that should have been modified according to circumstances, but it does underline the inflexibility of higher command and the difficulties and lapses of time involved in sending orders to all those concerned through the chain of command. Too often in our wargames, units act independently of each other and with astonishing manoeuvreability. In truth, once committed to action there was little a commander could do to change the orders of individual units.

Finally, it is interesting to note that Kershaw gives the reason for field and staff officers going on foot as being the nature of the terrain; this might be so but it was usual for officers who wanted to increase their chances of survival to dismount in the attack. During Pickett's charge, Garnett, injured by a kick from his horse, was the only officer to go in mounted, and was the first to fall. Of course, such heroes on horseback commanded the admiration of their men and could control the fighting better, but only if they could survive long enough!

Élite Troops

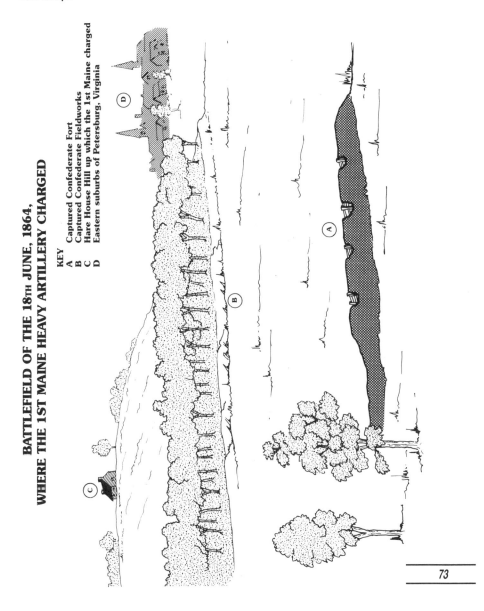

BATTLEFIELD OF THE 18TH JUNE, 1864,
WHERE THE 1ST MAINE HEAVY ARTILLERY CHARGED

KEY
A   Captured Confederate Fort
B   Captured Confederate Fieldworks
C   Hare House Hill up which the 1st Maine charged
D   Eastern suburbs of Petersburg, Virginia

The charge of the 1st Maine heavies at Petersburg was a disaster – within minutes, the regiment lost more than 600 of its 900 men. In a later attack on the Petersburg lines, the 4th New York Heavy Artillery found itself unsupported by neighbouring veteran units and, like the 1st Maine, was repulsed with heavy losses. It becomes obvious that these heavy artillery regiments had high morale but, more to the point, were well drilled.

At Cold Harbour in 1864, the 8th New York heavies managed to get within 20 feet of the enemy works with a loss of 505 men. The 7th New York was one of the few units actually to penetrate the Rebel position and, being artillerymen, turned the enemy's captured guns on their former owners. The 164th New York Zouaves (Irish), was another unit to get into the Confederate works at Cold Harbour – indeed, the several Zouave units of the Army of the Potomac in 1864 performed noticeably well in combat. It would seem their colourful garb made them feel like élite troops, as one member of the Zouave Brigade recalled:

'The outfits boosted the men's morale. We had the vanity to think there was no organisation in the army superior to us.'

In the fighting at Sanders' Field in the Wilderness, the 140th and 146th New York Zouaves continued to charge when the rest of their brigade, including the regulars, had fallen back to cover – losing 567 out of 1,600 men.

Élite regiments were not recruited in America as they were in Europe, rather they were born in the fire of battle. But if one unit can be said to be a 'corps d'élite', then it was Berdan's Sharpshooters. Two regiments were formed in 1861 and the qualification for entry was to place ten consecutive shots within 5 inches of the 'bull's eye' at a range of 200 yards. Initial armament was a Colt revolving rifle which proved dangerous to use and was replaced in May 1862 by the Sharps rifle. Individuals were also armed with long-range rifles with telescopic sights – even the chaplain was a crack shot and actually fought with such a rifle on the skirmish line at Chancellorsville. The Sharpshooters more often fought as detachments and were used mainly for reconnaissance, though they did fight as a brigade at Malvern Hill and Chancellorsville. The Sharpshooters are reputed to have shot more Confederates than any other unit. Yet even the Sharpshooters bowed to that other famous corps of the Army of the Potomac – The 'Iron Brigade'. One of Berdan's officers recalled seeing them after Chancellorsville:

'. . . that famed body of troops marching up that long muddy hill, unmindful of the pouring rain but full of life and spirit, with steady step, filling the entire roadway, their big black hats and feathers conspicuous . . . a model American volunteer.'

The Iron Brigade earned their reputation the hard way. Only the 2nd Wisconsin had seen action at First Bull Run when the brigade entered its first fight at Groveton in 1862. This regiment, over the length of the war, was to have the terrible distinction of the highest percentage losses of any unit of the Union Army. At Groveton, it took 500 men into the field and left 298 of them there as casualties. Altogether the brigade lost 751 out of 1,900 men. Green as they were, they held their positions in a stand-up, point-blank firefight against some of Jackson's finest infantry. They lost 149 men at Second Bull Run and 318 at Turner's Gap. By Antietam, the Western brigade was known as the 'Iron Brigade' and at that battle lost 342 out of 800 men. At Gettysburg the brigade lost 1,200 men out of 1,800. In the Wilderness, the brigade lost 902 men – the 2nd Wisconsin now down to 100 men was assigned to the provost guard. The Iron Brigade finished the war as the 6th and 7th Wisconsin and the 91st New York Heavy

☆☆☆☆☆☆	Yorktown.
☆☆☆☆	Fair Oaks.
☆☆☆☆	Gaine's Hill.
☆☆☆☆☆☆	Allen's Farm.
☆☆☆☆	Savage's Station.
☆☆☆☆	White Oak Bridge.
☆☆☆☆☆	Glendale.
	Malvern Hills.
	Antietam.
	69ᵀᴴ REGIMENT N.Y.S.V.
	IRISH BRIGADE
	Fredericksburg. Chancellorsville.
	Gettysburg. Bristoe's Station.

Flag of 69th New York Volunteers. 2nd National colour, 1864; Lettering – Gold.

Artillery; new drafts were received from Wisconsin bringing its strength up to 3,000 men. What made the Iron Brigade so good? For a start, it was relentlessly drilled to perfection by a regular army martinet by the name of Gibbon; it was composed of Westerners who had everything to prove in an army of Yankees; and, last but not least, the men were made to feel special by being issued distinctive dress uniforms and white gaiters – whilst almost all the other soldiers wore the kepi, the Westerners retained the tall Hardee dress hat complete with feathers as field wear.

In the Confederate armies, too, crack organisations developed. Particular states had a reputation for hard-fighting troops, notably Mississippi, Louisiana and Texas. Both the Army of Tennessee and the Army of Northern Virginia had tough Texas brigades. Hood's Texas Brigade in the Army of Northern Virginia became known as 'Lee's Grenadier Guard' – their fearless charges at Gaines' Mill, Antietam and the Wilderness completely

Flag of 52nd New York Volunteers.
Field – White; Eagle – Golden brown; Figure – Maroon cap and gown; Figure's flag – National colours with green laurel wreath; Oak leaves – Green and gold; Battle honours – Gold.

rocked the Federals. In a close study of the unit positions given on the battle maps in *The Gleam of Bayonets*, by J. V. Murfin, it is very evident just how effective was Hood's Texans' attack (which broke several brigades of Federal infantry). When Taylor's Brigade – the renowned 'Louisiana Tigers' – joined Jackson in the Shenandoah Valley in 1862 they were described as:

'Over 3,000 strong, neat in fresh clothing of grey with white gaiters, bands playing at the head of their regiments – not a straggler . . .'

At this time his Virginians were notorious stragglers and Jackson remarked to Taylor 'You must teach my people – they straggle badly.' The other brigade of Louisiana troops, known as the 'Pelicans', had an equally notable combat record.

CAVALRY VERSUS INFANTRY

Although Civil War cavalry was not used on the battlefield in large bodies until the end of the war (only in the case of the Union), it still had a role to play; if only a desperate one. On several occasions, Union commanders sacrificed a body of cavalry in order to retrieve themselves from difficulty.

At Gaines' Mill in 1862, Hood's Texans had broken through the Union line. In an effort to stem their advance, the 5th United States Cavalry was launched on a charge across 250 yards of open ground. The Texans, covered by timber, simply halted and opened fire. Only 100 riders returned out of the 250 that charged. At Cedar Mountain in 1862, the 1st Pennsylvania Cavalry delivered a charge with one of its battalions against a North Carolina brigade which was advancing in three scattered lines. This was a more opportune charge than that made at Gaines' Mill because the infantry were not ready to receive the attack. Nevertheless, the cavalry lost 93 men out of 164. The infantry lost 100 men during the course of the battle (having already fought a mêlée against a brigade of Federals), so we can assume the casualties caused by the cavalry charge were very light.

One interesting observation here is that the North Carolina skirmishers made themselves immune to swinging cavalry sabres by flinging themselves to the ground as the troopers galloped through them. Artillery men used similar tactics, crawling under guns and limbers. In most wargames, if the skirmishers or gunners failed to evade they would be seriously cut up – apparently this was not so in fact.

A final example of a desperate charge is to be found at Chancellorsville. The 8th Pennsylvania charged one battalion along a narrow track in the woods against Jackson's oncoming infantry in order to gain some time for the Federal batteries to reorganise, having just been ridden over by fleeing mule trains. The advance was checked momentarily with a loss of 3 officers, 30 men and 80 horses. This is a revealing statistic in that it indicates the vulnerability of horses to firearms – being bigger targets they are more likely to be hit. In a wargame it may be reasonable to assume that, although casualties on a cavalry unit will be perhaps 50% greater than those sustained by infantry, half the total losses could be returned as dismounted cavalry-men. One of the silliest cavalry charges ordered was that of Farnsworth's brigade by General Kilpatrick (or 'Killcavalry' as he was known). This charge was ordered against the Confederate right flank at Gettysburg, across rough terrain and against an enemy line posted behind fences. The charge took one of Law's Alabama regiments so completely by surprise that its first volley went over the heads of the charging troopers. After causing some initial disconcertation among the Rebels, the troopers rode back, minus Farnsworth and 100 men, most of them from the 300-strong 1st Vermont.

The Confederate cavalry also made a few desperate charges during the war – notably Bee's brigade at Pleasant Hill in 1864, one regiment losing a third of its men. But, generally speaking, the Confederates were more frugal in their use of cavalry. Members of Stuart's cavalry admitted to Major Freemantle (an observer from Britain) that they never charged the Federal infantry. The Confederate trooper brought his own horse to war and deigned to risk it, with the possibility of having to serve on foot if his mount was lost. Normally, the government would not replace a mount unless it died of wounds received in battle. When the Confederate cavalry did charge infantry, it was under favourable circumstances. At First Bull Run, J. E. B. Stuart's 250 Virginia cavalry charged out from behind an oak thicket into the unsuspecting 11th New York Zouaves whilst they were reforming from an attack on Henry Hill. The zouaves broke ranks and offered a scattering volley, emptying a few saddles only as they went through their ranks. Clearly, the charge had unnerved the zouaves who broke moments later when the batteries they were supporting fell to Confederate infantry.

In a skirmish at Cedarville, the 9th Virginia Cavalry charged in column down a road with one squadron and a squadron on each flank in the fields to either side of the road. The Federal infantry (1st Maryland – 1,000 men, plus two guns), had just been disordered by their own fleeing cavalry, and were attempting to deploy into line when the Rebel troopers struck. The column on the road was checked but the other two squadrons went in amongst the crowded and milling mass of infantry. The Federals lost 32 killed, 122 wounded and 600 captured. The Confederates, with 250 troopers, lost 11 killed and 15 wounded. In any wargame where cavalry can get to grips with infantry, the above contest should serve as a good yardstick from which to adjudicate an outcome. The important factor in this was, of course, the disorganisation of the Federals, which gave the Rebels the confidence to charge.

Again, in similar circumstances, following Shiloh, the 77th Ohio Infantry were ridden down by Confederate cavalry shooting carbines and revolvers. Their commander reported:

'We had no time to fix bayonets and were forced to fall back under cover of our cavalry.'

A popular myth exists which assumes that infantry in line could beat off attacking cavalry. As has already been pointed out, Civil War muskets were not that much more effective than those of Napoleonic times. Infantry still faced the same dangers from cavalry if they were unsupported in the open. The main difference lay in the tactical doctrines of commanders in relation to cavalry. Napoleonic commanders used their cavalry on the battlefield in conjunction with infantry and artillery. Civil War commanders kept their cavalry away from the main battle zone. They used cavalry as scouts and mounted raiders. When Phil Sheridan took command of the Army of the Potomac's cavalry, he completely revised this thinking. Grant wanted to send him off on various raids as was usual, but Sheridan persuaded him that the cavalry could serve the cause better if used alongside the infantry in battle. This he had demonstrated on many occasions during the Valley Campaign of 1864 and especially at Cedar Creek – admittedly the Confederates were outnumbered well over two to one most of the time, but Sheridan even had his troopers charging whilst mounted, the enemy behind breastworks. The cavalry arm of the Army of the Potomac came of age under Hooker in the spring of 1863, when he organised it into a properly constituted corps. However because Hooker preferred sending his cavalry off on raids in emulation of J. E. B. Stuart he lost the Battle of Chancellorsville in large part due to the fact that he had sent off nearly all of his cavalry on a fruitless raid. Similarly, Lee lost at Gettysburg because he did not have his cavalry with him and was unaware of the enemy dispositions.

At Gettysburg the Union cavalry played a major role in holding off the Confederate infantry at McPherson's Ridge, with their carbines on foot and supported by horse artillery until their infantry arrived. At the end of the fighting on the first day with two Union Corps in flight towards Gettysburg and Cemetery Hill, Buford threatened to charge the infantry of General Ewell with his division mounted. Part of Ewell's Corps was formed into squares in echelon to receive Buford. Buford did not charge, as he had created the desired effect in halting Ewell's pursuit. On a smaller scale, there are other isolated examples of infantry forming square when threatened by cavalry. At First Bull Run, with their army in rout, the 7th and 71st New York and the Regulars formed square to hold off the pursuing Confederate cavalry. At the battle of Ocean Pond, the raw 64th Georgia infantry was formed into square as unsupported, its colonel felt threatened by Union cavalry. At Five Forks a regiment of Confederate infantry went into a hollow square when it found mounted companies of Sheridan's troopers on its flank. I know of no instances when cavalry charged a formed square in the Civil War, but this possibility should remain as an outside chance in any wargame.

The fact that infantry rarely formed square was mainly due to the fact that cavalry rarely intervened in the infantry battle and, when they did, the infantry usually had some cover available which deterred a charge home. On other occasions, the action of enemy cavalry often neutralised any possible intervention of cavalry on the battlefield. When going into action against infantry, it was more usual for cavalry to dismount and fight on foot. The Union cavalrymen of Wilson's Corps were particularly effective with their Spencer repeaters at the Battle of Nashville when they fought on foot. Forrest's cavalry, too, most often fought on foot. At Brice's Crossroads, they walked forward in line, blasting the undergrowth with shotguns, pistols, carbines and rifles. Here too the Union cavalry, some of whom had Colt repeating rifles, also fought in the main on foot. Towards the end of the war Confederate cavalry armed themselves with rifles and fought mostly dismounted.

CAVALRY VERSUS CAVALRY

Cavalry Combat Performance

There is no doubt that, during the early part of the war,

the Confederate cavalry completely dominated their Union opponents through their superior horsemanship and better organisation; from the start an effort was made to group regiments of cavalry into brigades and divisions under their own very capable leaders. The Union cavalry was parceled out to the infantry corps and did not fight as part of a large formation. The formation of cavalry regiments was actively discouraged in the Union army; the commanders had no faith in horse soldiers as fighting men and used them as couriers and escorts and as guards to the trains. This attitude gave rise to the jibe, 'Who ever saw a dead cavalryman.'

The Union cavalry arm had little respect from the rest of the army and their enemies for a long time. They suffered poor arms and equipment and many regiments were armed with little more than a sabre. The cavalry recruits were mostly city dwellers and farmers who were not used to riding cavalry horses. The Confederate troopers were not unlike English Civil War Cavaliers. Many were gentlemen and sons of gentlemen who were used to

Flag of 8th New York Cavalry.
Field – Dark blue; Big scroll – Dark blue, edged gold; Lettering and cloud – White; Eagle – Brown and light blue; Eagle's scroll – Red; Stars – White; Fringe – Gold.

riding and equestrian sport. As a consequence, they were able to outride and outshoot the Union cavalry during the first two years of the war. That J. E. B. Stuart was able to ride completely around McClellan's army outside of Richmond in early 1862, illustrates the impotence of the Union cavalry and the ineptitude of its leaders. Cooke, Pleasonton, Stoneman and Averell were all very mediocre cavalry leaders when compared to the Confederate leaders – Stuart, Forrest, Ashby, Wheeler, Hampton, Morgan and Fitz Lee.

Although the Confederate troopers were of good stock, hardy and well led, they were undisciplined. The high-spirited troopers had little use for regulations and drill; besides they were constantly active, patrolling, raiding and guarding the communications etc. to have time to drill. Some of the Confederate cavalry leaders were ignorant of drill and discipline and knew nothing of formal tactics. Forrest was a natural-born leader and a fighter brave to excess. He lived by the maxim 'Get there first, with the most men' ('Get there fustest with the mostest', unfortunately being a distortion for effect – Forrest being semi-literate). Ashby, who commanded Jackson's cavalry in the first Valley campaigns, was equally daring and reckless, and equally ignorant of drill and discipline, though by the spring of 1862 he had learned something of tactics. Nevertheless, many Confederate troopers were allowed to come and go as they pleased at first and it took some time to change this attitude. By 1863 the cavalry of the main Confederate armies was a well disciplined force – units such as 1st, 2nd and 4th Virginia, 1st Mississippi, 1st Kentucky, 26th Texas and Hampton's Legion were exceptionally well drilled.

By the spring of 1863, the Union cavalry was becoming a force to be reckoned with. In the Army of the Potomac, Hooker had organised the cavalry into a proper corps command. Although it showed up badly at Kelly's Ford, mainly due to the apprehensions of Averell its commander, the Union troopers put up a marvellous fight in the biggest cavalry battle of the Civil War – Brandy Station on 9th June 1863, which involved 10,000 troopers on each side; the Federals lost 866 men and the Rebels 523. To get an idea of the proportions of casualties inflicted by cavalry on other cavalry, the following Federal regiments suffered the highest losses: 6th Pennsylvania, 146 out of 500; 1st New Jersey, 56 out of 280; 2nd U.S., 68 out of 225 men. Although some of these casualties were caused by dismounted carbine and artillery fire, most of the action was on horseback. When two opposing cavalry lines charged each other, the files would open out to allow opposing riders to pass through the formation. Very few casualties would occur in this pass through. When columns were used, the fighting was more deadly. At Rummel's Farm on 3rd July 1863, the Confederate cavalry attacked in a massive column of squadrons. General Custer led the 1st Michigan of his brigade smack into its head. A member of the 3rd Pennsylvania who witnessed the charge commented:

'As the columns approached each other the pace of each increased when suddenly a crash like the falling of timbers betokened the crisis. So sudden and violent was the collision that many of the horses were turned end over end and crushed their riders beneath them.'

Also during this battle, the 7th Michigan countercharged the crack 1st Virginia but was driven back with a loss of 13 killed, 48 wounded and 39 captured, out of 461 men. One Union cavalryman reported that the Confederate officers insisted that their men kept to their sabres for the mêlée; at Brandy Station they had called to the Union troopers: 'Draw your pistols and fight like gentlemen.' Apparently the Rebels had been impressed with the way in which the Federals had used their sabres. Brooke Rawle, a Union colonel wrote that Hampton's brigade came on: 'In close column of squadrons, advancing as if on review with sabres drawn.'

Sabres and Pistols

Although the Union cavalry favoured the sabre over the pistol for mêlée, there were many cavalry leaders who felt that the 'arm blanche' was no longer the best arm for the cavalryman. To use the sabre correctly and efficiently required a great deal of drill and training in its use, both on an individual level and as a formed body of cavalry. Perhaps this is one reason why the Confederates preferred the pistol and shotgun for mounted action. A well-delivered sabre charge, however, had the same psychological effect as an infantry bayonet charge, ie frightening the charged and encouraging the chargers to make contact. One European observer commenting on an action between the cavalry described the opposing horsemen as reigning in short of delivering a charge and 'making a noise with their carbines and pistols' and apparently causing few casualties. Although there were many exponents of the sabre, there were equally as many who favoured firearms for cavalry use. J. S. Mosby's company of the 1st Virginia Cavalry were issued sabres at the beginning of the war. Mosby wrote:

> 'I dragged one through the first year of the war but when I became a commander I discarded it.'

Mosby's Virginia Partisan Rangers did not carry sabres at all. Their style of fighting was that of guerillas who struck out of nowhere and dispersed to neighbouring homesteads having carried out their mission of sabotage, or whatever. For such close range, quick action, the revolver was the preferred weapon, of which each Ranger had at least two. Sabres were useless as they rarely had to face or make a regular mounted charge. Mosby commented:

> 'The sabre is of no use against gunpowder. My men were as little impressed by a body of cavalry charging with sabres as though they had been armed with cornstalks. I think that my command reached the highest point of efficiency as cavalry because they were well armed with two six-shooters and their charges combined the effect of fire and shock.'

On the Union side, General Wilson condemned the sabre as:

> '. . . out of date for cavalry in a country like ours as the short sword of the Roman soldier is for infantry. It is in the way and is of no value whatever in a fight, compared with repeating rifles, carbines and pistols.'

Despite Wilson's views, it was precisely one of his units, and mounted infantry at that, that delivered a convincing sabre charge on Forrest's command, wounding the man himself! This was carried out by the sabre battalion (four companies) of the 17th Indiana Mounted Infantry at Ebenezer Church, 1st April, 1865. The 1st and 2nd New York Mounted Rifles that served in the Army of the Potomac were also issued sabres in 1864, though it was not until later in the year that they received mounts, thus the Rifles had to drag their swords along as they 'foot-slogged' with the rest of the infantry. That sabres should be issued to such units at such a late stage in the war demonstrates that the arm blanche was indeed still a respected weapon in the right hands and in the right circumstances.

Lances

Compared to the sabre, the lance was far and away a more ludicrous weapon for Civil War cavalry operating in mainly wooded terrain. To use a lance required additional training, and few volunteers were managing to grasp the essentials of sabre drill, let alone learn to cope with a lance as well. The 6th Pennsylvania Cavalry did in fact carry a lance, right up until two weeks before the Battle of Brandy Station, when they drew Sharps carbines instead. The 6th, along with the 1st New York (Veteran) Regiment was the finest volunteer regiment in the Army of the Potomac. According to a staff officer of Stuart, the Lancers broke and fled before a charge of Confederate cavalry in 1862. Certainly their lances were never bloodied in combat. Some units of Texas cavalry equipped themselves with lances in emulation of the Mexican cavalry. On the plains, lancers could be effective. At Valverde, at least one unit, the 5th Texas Mounted Rifles, was armed with lances and charged with them, on foot too. Later, the 21st, 24th, 25th and 26th Regiments of Texas Cavalry were raised and armed with lances.

CAVALRY VERSUS ARTILLERY

The great cavalry battle at Brandy Station in 1863, featured several charges by mounted troopers on deployed batteries of artillery – some successful, some not. Cavalry could often manoeuvre into a position on the flank of a battery from whence they could charge to effect. During the battle, Buford's Union cavalry was checked in its initial charge against Hart's Confederate horse artillery. When the battery supports, the 6th and 7th Virginia, were driven off, Hart was forced to withdraw firing by prolonge. Their canister forced Buford's men to cover. Later in the morning the 6th United States and 6th Pennsylvania charged against Beckham's Battery of Stuart's Horse Artillery. Major Hart, commanding the guns described their charge:

'The charge was made over a plateau fully eight hundred yards wide, and the objective point was the artillery at the church. Never rode troopers more gallantly than did those steady regulars, as under a fire of shell and shrapnel, and finally of canister, they dashed up to the very muzzles, then through and beyond our guns, passing between Hampton's left and Jones' right. Here they were simultaneously attacked from both flanks and the survivors driven back.'

Beckham's gunners were soon back at their pieces without suffering loss; they shelled the woods in front, where the Federals were massing. In most wargames rules I know of, gunners would have suffered grievous losses at the hands of cavalry, yet the fact is artillerymen, like skirmishers, fell flat on their faces to avoid sabre blows and had the added protection afforded by diving under guns and wagons. J. C. Wise commented:

'. . . gunners will always possess a great advantage in the brief hand to hand conflict which will ensue, for the majority of the mounted men will, as a rule, pass on through the guns, unable to draw rein.'

If cavalry did get in among artillery, then severe casualties amongst the crew could be expected. This again happened at Brandy Station; Martin's Battery of 3 guns deployed on the slope of Fleetwood Hill across which a good deal of the action took place, when the 35th Virginia Battalion charged with two squadrons and came around the West side of the hill taking the gunners by surprise and driving off the cavalry supports. The Union gunners stood firm. Martin reported on the action:

'Once in the battery it became a hand to hand fight with pistol and sabre between the enemy and my cannoneers and drivers, and never did the men act with more coolness and bravery and show more of a stern purpose to do their duty unflinchingly, and above all to save their guns: and while the loss of them is a matter of great regret to me, it is a consolation and great satisfaction to know that I can point with pride to the fact that, of those little band who defended the battery not one of them flinched for a moment from his duty. Of the 36 men I took into the engagement but 6 came out safely . . .'

Several other charges were made on guns during the battle. Those that were successful were made against the flanks. Several frontal attacks were made by both sides against artillery which were repulsed.

At Gettysburg, near Rummel's Farm, two Union batteries fired into Hampton's troopers. W. E. Miller, 3rd Pennsylvania Cavalry, describes the attack:

'. . . there appeared moving towards us a large mass of cavalry . . . They were formed in close column of squadrons . . . They marched with well-aligned fronts and steady reins. Their polished sabre blades dazzled in the sun. Shell and shrapnel met the advancing Confederates and tore through their ranks. Closing the gaps as if nothing had happened, on they came. As they drew nearer, canister was substituted by our gunners for shell, and horse after horse staggered and fell. Still they came on. Our mounted skirmishers rallied and fell, into line; the dismounted men fell back, and a few of them reached their horses. The 1st Michigan, drawn up in close column of squadrons near Pennington's battery, was ordered by Gregg to charge. Custer, who was near, placed himself at its head, and off they dashed.'

Following Gettysburg, at Williamsport, Imboden's cavalry brigade with twenty-two guns held off five regular and eight volunteer regiments of Union cavalry, as the main Confederate army escaped to friendly territory across the Potomac. On this occasion, the Union troopers attacked on foot. The artillery, well down on ammunition, kept them at bay, while Imboden made up a scratch force of infantry from the 500 drivers that were with the column of wagons he was escorting. He kept the wagonners moving up and down the reverse slope of the hill he defended, showing them first at one point and then at another. The ruse was sufficient to deter any serious Union charge which if de-livered would have overrun his position. Stuart then arrived with 3,000 troopers to attack the Union rear.

INFANTRY VERSUS ARTILLERY

The backbone of any line of defence was its artillery-firing canister, preferably from 12 pounder Napoleons. General Hill commented that the Confederate infantry and the Union artillery side by side 'need fear no foe on earth.' It is true that the Confederates fought their battles with infantry and the Union preferred to confront their furious attacks with artillery, leading one Union soldier to comment that, 'there is one thing that I like about this army . . . we fight our battles with artillery whereas the Rebels fight theirs with infantry – like a man's life ain't worth a cent.'

Examples of Confederate charges upon Union gun lines are numerous. In most cases, even though the infantry supports often fled, the gunners remained staunchly in defence of their pieces. At 2nd Bull Run, Benning's Georgia Brigade charged; 'Blue regiments on the far bank fired on ragged volley then turned and fled up the slope.' The charge failed to clear a supporting battery which, firing canister, brought the Georgians to a halt at the bed of a creek within 65 yards of the guns, where they found shelter from their fire. As testament to the effectiveness of canister fire consider these statistics: Gaines' Mill, 1862, the 20th North Carolina charged a battery on McGhee's Hill and lost 70 killed and 200 wounded; the 12th North Carolina and the 3rd Alabama in support and charging another battery, lost 212 and 200 men each respectively. In the same battle, Whiting's Division (2 brigades), took 1020 casualties before overrunning 14 Union guns. The crack 4th Texas, leading the assault, was the first to pierce the line with a total loss of 250 men. At Antietam, the 9th New York lost 221 men in an effort to take a four gun battery less than 200 yards from their position. At Petersburg, the 4th New York Heavy Artillery received 115 casualties in an unsuccessful charge on two emplaced Rebel guns.

Claims that the overall percentage of casualties inflicted by artillery was small can be misleading. As Colonel Wise pointed out, the soldiers usually had sense enough to give canister-firing batteries a wide berth; if not, casualties could be horrendous, as outlined above. However, at Malvern Hill the Union artillery inflicted 50% of the total Confederate casualties, 'an unprecedented thing in war' according to D. H. Hill. At this battle, one of Hill's brigades managed to advance only half way across the 900 yards of open ground before they were forced to find sparse shelter in the furrows of a ploughed field. (Interestingly, the Confederate infantry replied with their muskets at this long range – ie 450 yards!)

Union column crosses ford covered by 12 pdr Napoleon battery.
(*Photograph by Stephen Foulk*)

In many of the big battles of the war, the Union managed to concentrate many batteries in defensive positions upon which Confederate attacks were smashed. Malvern Hill has already been cited. At Shiloh, also in 1862, the Federals organised a last-ditch stand, with a grand battery of field artillery supplemented by a battery of 30 pounders, on high ground at Dill's Branch. Although supported by only two regiments of infantry, this line of defence kept the Confederates from driving the Union army into the Tennessee River. At Antietam, the artillery of several corps was posted north of the infamous 'cornfield' and supported by fire from long-range rifles across the Creek, blasted the Rebels in the corn, heralding Hooker's attack. Later in the morning the gun line served as a rallying point for the broken Union regiments. At Chancellorsville, the Federals deployed twenty guns at Hazel Grove which checked Stonewall Jackson's onslaught with canister. When the Union right collapsed at Stones' River, massed artillery at the Round Wood prevented any further Rebel advance and offered a rallying point for routed units. On the second day of this battle, 58 guns stopped Breckinridge's attack before the Rebels had got much further than half way to them.

A similar situation was to be seen at 2nd Bull Run: this time the Confederates deployed two massed batteries (16 and 24 guns), behind their main infantry position – the Union attackers could not get any closer than 200 yards to the Confederate line. At 1st Bull Run, the Confederate defence consisted of some 20 guns deployed on the reverse of a hill, lining a pine thicket. It was unusual for the Confederates to employ massed batteries in defence. In the two quoted examples, their guns were well back off the front line or hidden from view. Because of the superior weight and numbers of the Federal artillery, the Rebels tended to keep their guns under cover. At Antietam, their centre was held by artillery only and many guns were hidden in folds in the ground. When the Federal infantry attacked, the guns were brought into action at close range.

In the offence, Confederate artillery was sometimes used *en masse*, as at Gettysburg on both the second and third days. Longstreet assembled 60 guns at the Peach Orchard position, arranged in a great arc up to 10,000 yards from the Union lines, and opened on them a destructive fire before the main infantry assault. An even greater concentration of guns was seen the following day – the biggest of the war in fact – when 142 Confederate guns bombarded the Union position on Cemetery Ridge. The Confederate fire was most ineffective. Many projectiles passed harmlessly over the heads of the defenders. Artillery officers, such as Brown and Dance of the Confederate 2nd Corps, attributed the ineffectiveness of this fire to the poor quality of their shells. In fact, solid shot was mostly used, as many shells failed to explode and hence were no better than shot but without the weight and ricochet effect. Indeed, the Confederate bombardment at Gettysburg was so disappointing that such large concentrations of artillery were never seen again in the war. Burnside experienced similar frustration when he attempted to clear out defending Confederates from Fredricksburg. Even his 20 and 30 pounder guns could make little impression, as the Rebels hid in cellars until the bombardment ceased.

In the offence, artillery was sometimes brought right up to the front line to fire canister. An early example of this tactic was at First Bull Run where two Union batteries were brought up to fight on the front line on the Henry Hill. A Confederate regiment of some 400 men approached the guns and, because they wore blue, were taken to be the battery supports promised. At a range of 70 yards the 33rd Virginia unleashed a volley on the batteries mowing down 40 gunners and 75 horses in the nearest battery alone. (Note that the amount of horses hit was twice that of the gunners – they were bigger and closer order targets – similarly in counter-battery fire horses suffered far worse casualties than the gunners and rules should take this into consideration.) Such early experiences tended to put artillerists off the idea of offensive tactics at close range. Nevertheless Hooker brought up several batteries to blast the 'cornfield' with canister at Antietam and Ruggles at Shiloh assembled massed batteries in front of the 'Hornet's Nest' in an attempt to reduce the opposition with canister fire. On a smaller scale, Pelham, the Confederate Horse Artillery genius, tried unlimbering guns within yards of the firing line on at least two occasions. At Spotsylvania, a section of Union artillery was brought right up to the Rebel works to fire canister but the gunners were 'shot down in short order.'

ARTILLERY VERSUS ARTILLERY

It has already been noted that the Union artillery was superior in every respect to that of the Confederates. At Malvern Hill, the Confederates attempted to prepare the way for their infantry assaults by bringing up guns through the woods. As they deployed, the Union guns concentrated first on one, then another battery, forcing the grey gunners to relinquish the fight. Because of the accuracy of the rifled guns, counter-battery fire was a more realistic proposition in the Civil War than it had been in Napoleon's time. However, following Malvern Hill, the Rebels rarely squared up against the Union artillery. Gettysburg was the exception. The Union army fighting defensively had their guns more dispersed and naturally the Confederates could concentrate their guns at the point of attack.

During their reply to the Rebel bombardment, the Union guns were more effective in an anti-personnel role. Before Pickett's attack had even started, his division had lost 300 men to 25 guns. Despite their high trajectory, the Rebel guns disabled about a dozen Union guns on Cemetery Ridge. At Antietam, it was the Confederate artillery that was severely punished by long range fire to which they could offer no effective reply – the battle was known as 'Artillery Hell.'

6   COMMANDERS

GENERALS

Any evaluation of the competency or otherwise of historical generalship can only be subjective. Just what do we evaluate? Can we class generals according to their tactical doctrines, and ignore experience and personality, or is it enough to say they were above or below average? Some generals were consistent in their behaviour. Others (more often those of political appointment) were apt to be less predictable. Some generals led from the front (and lost control of the battle in most cases), others sent out their orders realising that the troops they had committed were largely out of their control but that proper use of reserves and timing was not. Some generals had great personal energy and could be seen at all points of danger rallying and encouraging their soldiers. Some had a lot less stamina through poor health or past wounds. Others were just bone idle or drunkards.

With such a multiplicity of factors to consider, it is difficult therefore to give a comprehensive classification of types of general. Finally, the type of classification desired must have a place in the rules one uses and obviously the more classifications, the more complex the rules. If subordinate generals are not considered as characters, then those not directly controlled by subordinate players in a multiplayer game become telepathic and too easily controlled by the commander-in-chief.

EVALUATION OF ARMY COMMANDERS

United States Army	Charisma	Reliability	Aggression
U. S. Grant	6	9	7
W. T. Sherman	7	9	6
G. B. McClellan	9	9	4
H. W. Halleck	4	9	4
I. McDowell	4	5	5
D. C. Buell	6	5	8
W. S. Rosecrans	7	8	6
J. Pope	3	3	7

A. E. Burnside	5	3	5
J. Hooker	7	6	4
G. H. Thomas	7	8	5
G. G. Meade	4	7	5
J. B. McPherson	8	9	7
E. O. C. Ord	6	6	5
N. F. Lyon	9	6	9
F. Sigel	9	5	3
N. P. Banks	6	4	4
B. F. Butler	5	5	5
J. C. Fremont	7	3	4
D. Hunter	4	5	8
P. H. Sheridan	8	8	9
S. R. Curtis	6	8	6
Confederate States Army			
R. E. Lee	10	9	9
J. E. Johnston	8	9	5
A. S. Johnston	10	6	9
B. Bragg	5	7	9
E. Van Dorn	8	5	9
J. C. Pemberton	7	7	6
E. K. Smith	8	8	8
J. B. Hood	8	7	10
T. L. Jackson	9	8	8
J. Longstreet	7	9	6
L. Polk	9	6	7
W. J. Hardee	5	9	6
P. G. T. Beauregard	8	7	5
J. A. Early	5	7	10
S. Price	9	7	8
J. C. Breckinridge	9	7	8
H. H. Sibley	5	6	6
B. McCulloch	6	9	5
F. K. Zollicoffer	8	5	9
J. E. B. Stuart	10	7	7
N. B. Forrest	10	8	10

Note: attributes of charisma, reliability and aggression are scored on a scale of ten.

Charisma. Personal magnetism of the officer, how well he can inspire, rally his troops. His presence will be of morale value. In wargames, generals usually have to be with a unit to gain full moral benefit. But, General Lee on two occasions during the

Virginia Campaign of 1864 had to be forcibly turned back by troops he was attempting to lead into action in desperate circumstances!

Reliability. How trustworthy was the officer concerned? At Gettysburg, Sickles, a political general, moved his corps to a forward position without authorisation from Meade, his C-in-C, endangering the whole army as a result. At the same battle, Hood disobeyed instructions from Longstreet to obey Lee's orders to attack up the Emmitsburg Road. Instead, he went for the Round Top and Devil's Den positions and almost rolled up the Union left. The question is, was Hood a reliable officer if he did not sometimes obey orders? Perhaps he could be relied upon to use his discretion? In a wargame, then, a subordinate may be allowed to use his discretion simply by allowing the player commanding the model army to change any previous order to accommodate a change in circumstances. However, it is unlikely that a timid general would respond to a change of circumstances in an aggressive way, just as an aggressive general like Hood would act cautiously.

Aggression. By and large, Confederate generals adopted offensive tactics right up until 1864, when the lack of resources and manpower threw them onto the defensive. Confederate generals were also more likely to actually lead their troops from the front, at great personal risk.

Using Generals' Characteristics in Wargames
When any of the generals' attributes of charisma, reliability or aggression are required, throw a ten-sided die. If the score equals or is less than their rating on the above tables, they may apply that characteristic to the wargame situation arising. In morale tests, generals may add one to morale scores of units under their control. When orders are written, dice for each general's reliability. Those that prove unreliable, dice again on the aggression table. Units commanded by generals which exceed their aggression rating, advance cautiously if given orders to attack or otherwise hold or defend. Unreliable generals that prove to be aggressive, change hold orders to 'cautious attack' and all other orders to 'attack'. Reliable generals may be allowed to change the orders of their units once only in a game, in the manner of either an aggressive or cautious general, at the discretion of the player.

7 CAMPAIGNS

Organising Campaigns

Good campaigns are not only difficult to organise, they are difficult to co-ordinate and require much of the umpire's or organiser's time and patience to keep their momentum going. In my experience, most wargamers try to walk before they can run when it comes to running a campaign – they are very often too ambitious in scope and detail. Who plays in the campaign is most important, for it is no use in having half-interested parties involved, or butterflies who can't settle to concentrate on any one theme for a prolonged period. Continuity is important, and players will often lose interest if the campaign is intermittently conducted. Quite often, a small group of dedicated players is better than many superficially-interested players who can't be relied upon to turn up for campaign games or forget to send in orders. Boredom is the death knell of any campaign and it is no easy job to ensure that every player in the campaign is totally involved for most of the time – after all, this is recreation not real war.

That said, campaigns are usually more successful if their aims and objectives are limited and easily defined. To attempt to tackle the whole war and include economic and political factors, as well as military facets, might be beyond the scope of any one campaign organiser. The organiser must decide what is the main theme of the campaign and subordinate other factors to this. Most wargamers tend to prefer the military aspects of a wargame – they would not be wargamers otherwise. It has also been suggested by some that diplomacy is particularly enjoyed by many as a diversion from regular wargaming.

The theatre of war could be broadened out to Mexico, perhaps with France entering the war from the south; or to Canada, where British troops cross the border in recognition of the Confederacy. There were many interesting amphibious operations during the Civil War where naval and land forces can be used in close proximity – this might inspire some to model vessels to figure scale and/or fight the bigger naval battles with much smaller models. Landing parties of sailors and marines may even be added to wargames collections, as might coastal artillery and

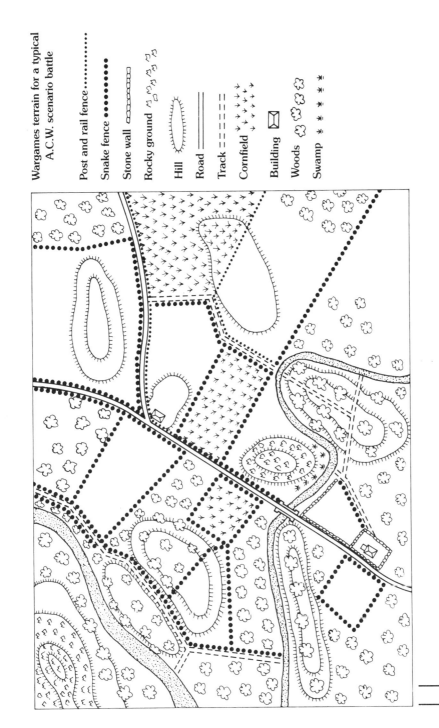

Wargames terrain for a typical A.C.W. scenario battle

Post and rail fence ....
Snake fence ● ● ● ● ●
Stone wall ⊂▭▭▭▭▭⊃
Rocky ground
Hill
Road ══════
Track ═ ═ ═ ═ ═
Cornfield
Building
Woods
Swamp

segments of fortresses. Several campaigns were fought to take major cities such as Atlanta, Vicksburg and Petersburg – again, other interesting items of wargames paraphernalia would have to be acquired that are not usually employed in field actions, for example, mortars, engineers, siege equipment, railways and field defences. Sibley's Campaign in New Mexico could make an interesting campaign piece for three players, one taking the Indians or perhaps a fourth party taking a role using Mexicans. The Valley Campaigns of Stonewall Jackson and Jube Early are ideal for campaigns, being geographically contained. A while ago, I tried a Union cavalry raid with two columns sent deep into Southern Territory. The contestant players each commanded a column and had to perform against each other alternately against a third party (myself) commanding the Confederate forces, through a series of scenarios. Board games lend themselves as ready-made campaign games, from which battle contacts can be resolved with figure games in perhaps a less abstract way. Some wargamers have fought their way through the war, recreating all the major battles. In a similar vein, a series of battle fields can be drawn up as alternatives to those that followed in historical chronology. Finally, solo campaigns allow a wargamer to really indulge himself, maybe inviting friends in to play the part of an enemy commander when convenient, and taking time over details which might prove tedious or uninteresting to less dedicated gamers.

Some Basic Campaign Details

Before embarking on a campaign, it is as well to have an idea of a few of the essentials required in the formulation of rules or guidelines.

Wagons. In the Napoleonic Wars, an average of 12 wagons per 1,000 men was usual but, in America where vast areas of the country were scarcely inhabited, the armies had to carry their provisions with them. The Shenandoah Valley was an important invasion route because of its foraging potential. When McClellan invaded the Virginia Peninsula, he had 5,000 wagons for 110,000 men. At Fredricksburg, Burnside had 50 wagons per 1,000 men. With such high ratios of wagons to men, the army could operate from its main supply base for a period of 10 days.

At Chancellorsville, Hooker had 33 wagons per 1,000 troops, allowing at most 6 days travel from his railhead; in their haversacks, his men carried 11 days rations, almost double the usual quota. Dessicated vegetables, introduced in March 1863, allowed this greater quantity to be carried. According to Meade's orders of August 1863, a regiment of 500 men was allowed 4 commissary wagons and 1 hospital wagon. Brigade HQs had 3 wagons, division HQs had 5 wagons and corps HQs had 11 wagons. A 6-gun Napoleon battery required 6 ammunition wagons; a similar 10 pdr, Rifled battery would require 2, and a 20 pounder battery of 4 guns, 6 wagons. The ambulance train consisted of 3 ambulances to every regiment in the corps. Additionally each brigade had 1 medicine wagon and 1 army wagon.

Supply depot and wagon park. (*Photograph by Stevie Willis*)

Marching. An average of 9 to 12 miles was considered a normal day's march for an army, though smaller detachments might march further or force march over double the normal distances. Foot soldiers jettisoned much equipment as they marched. In the Union army, 25% of the soldiers discarded their knapsacks and made do with a blanket roll. Confederates were rarely issued knapsacks anyway – about 25% made use of knapsacks, captured or issued and the rest used the blanket roll to contain their belongings. Most soldiers retained their canteens and haversacks.

Orders of march had to be carefully worked out before the army moved, and each commander had to be aware of his unit's place in the column. Stonewall Jackson was so secretive that he often withheld the destination points from his commanders with, at times, the confusion and frayed tempers that were an inevitable consequence. Without a proper time schedule, traffic jams could occur. This happened when Grant undertook a night march by his left flank – his chief lieutenants, Meade and Sheridan, clashed as the latter's cavalry blocked an important road to the infantry's objective.

Roads. Most roads in America at this time were little more than dirt tracks which were dusty in summer and quagmires in winter rains. Some of the more important highways were macadamised but these often fell into disrepair through continued use. The Valley Turnpike in Virginia's Shenandoah Valley, for example, was crumbling and pot-holed for much of its length at the end of the war. Roadways were particularly important to McClellan on the Peninsula when he attempted his change of base – the lowland roads had to be 'corduroyed' by engineers laying logs across their widths to bear the heavy traffic. At times, captured old muskets were used to corduroy. When Burnside attempted to march around Lee's flank after Fredricksburg, his army literally became stuck in the mud.

Railroads. Out of 30,000 miles of railroad in America only 9,000 lay within the Confederate States. Variable rail gauges caused delays – Richmond, for example, was the railhead for 5 tracks. Military interference in the realms of railroad executives exacerbated the problems of running to time table with, at times, tragic results. The Union soon employed Haupt as chief of the military railroad, which helped matters greatly. The Confederates were less efficient and preferred to retain civilian control of their railroads until it was too late.

Locomotive speeds were determined by track condition rather than by engine capacity. As the war continued, the Confederacy's railroads fell into disrepair. On a good track a light train could make 60 mph and, if laden, 40 mph with 20 freight cars. The South did not have engine-building facilities and had to make do and mend. The North had 12 major centres of rail production.

As well as conveying supplies, the railroad was used decisively at First Bull Run where train-borne reinforcements tipped the scales of battle in favour of the Confederates. In 1863, the Confederates again used the railroad for the wholesale transference of troops to a critical theatre of the war when Longstreet's

Corps of the Army of Northern Virginia reinforced the Army of Tennessee for the Battle of Chickamauga; since Burnside's Union army was in occupation of Knoxville on the most direct route, a circuitous journey of 1,000 miles had to be made, taking ten days to accomplish.

Rivers. Moving supplies by river was a third cheaper than by rail and, where convenient, commanders availed themselves of this facility. Major campaigns were fought for control of the rivers Tennessee and Mississippi and their tributaries. These were successful for the Union, though Banks' Red River campaign ended in failure. As well as the Confederate gunboats, the Union soldiers and sailors detached to patrol the waterways had to suffer frequent raids and bankside harassment from Confederate guerillas. Jeff Thompson's guerillas caused particular annoyance to the Federals in Missouri and Mississippi. In Virginia, the rivers that ran roughly N.W. to S.E. formed natural barriers for any overland march on Richmond. Navigable for up to fifty miles in most places, these rivers figured largely in Grant's strategy to sidestep Confederate opposition to his left flank, where supply bases could aid the movement of his forces from positions considerably inland. McClellan, too, had used Virginia's waterways as invasion routes to the Confederate capital, though he took the more radical step of moving his entire army down the Chesapeake, supplying it from Fort Monroe and then from West Point on the York River.

Intelligence. Reports of enemy activity or intentions came in various forms. Pinkerton is perhaps the most famous intelligence officer of the civil war, but he grossly overestimated the strength of the Confederate forces opposing McClellan which led that commander to be extremely cautious when instead he could have captured Richmond in 1862. Some spies were specifically recruited by the government but others came into spying through chance; some, like 17 year-old Belle Boyd, fed Stonewall Jackson much useful information. It was quite easy for spies of both sides to mix freely with enemy troops without detection by language differences. For the most part, Confederate generals were better supplied with intelligence from the sympathetic areas in which their armies generally operated.

This can be simulated in a wargames campaign by allowing armies operating on home ground to move faster and force an opponent to reveal his true strength when the armies are in close proximity. Cavalry, too, played an important part in gathering intelligence. Here again the Confederates had the advantage in having more effective cavalry, at least until 1865. The cavalry were effectively the eyes of the army. In the Gettysburg campaign, Stuart let Lee down badly when he went off on a glory ride at a considerable distance away from the main army, with the Confederate cavalry. Some wargamers sneer at the idea of scouting mechanisms in terms of points values attributed to cavalry type and quality, but the fact is many battles commenced with a cavalry action. If time permits, cavalry contacts can be fought out on the wargames table using skirmish rules. Again, in a wargame before deploying the main forces of each side, a cavalry encounter could preclude the main battle with the defeated side forced to deploy first.

Losses. About 25% of the casualties were fatalities. Of the remainder a good 50% would be unlikely to return to duty. A defeated side would lose in addition about 25% of its losses in casualties as prisoners. Of course, these are very rough guidelines and circumstances did alter cases in actuality. Desertion was a major problem for both sides and was especially rife in the Confederate armies early in the war where regular discipline was not understood and the soldiers simply absented themselves for what they thought reasonable grounds. Harvest time caused a very noticeable drain of manpower. When Lee invaded the North in September 1862 he fielded 37,000 men – a staggering 20,000 had absented themselves but later rejoined their commands. In the Union armies, desertion was most prevalent in 1864, when many immigrants and draft substitutes came into the ranks. Many enlisted solely for the attractive bounties offered, immediately deserted and rejoined for another bounty in another state.

Signals. Invented by Morse in 1844, the telegraph saw much use. Its lines followed the direction of railroads and major highways. The first signal corps was introduced into the Union army.

The Federal Military Telegraph system was supervised by the Secretary of War, Stanton. The Confederates did not interfere with private civilian control of their telegraph system. (This attitude of decentralised government pervaded much of Davis' policies and ultimately was a major cause in the South's defeat.) By 1864, telegraphs were commonly used in the field and in Union armies every brigade had a telegraph detachment. Messages could be sent up to five miles via a field telegraph. The early Beardslee telegraphs were powered by a hand-cranked magneto but these were supplanted by heavier, battery-powered machines.

Other forms of signalling were conducted using flags, though semaphore was not used. Signal stations were built on mountains and in this way messages could be relayed over very long distances. At night, flares were substituted.

Balloons. Were used during 1862 and up to May 1863 when the Federal Balloon Corps was disbanded. The Balloon Corps was the brainchild of Lowe, a celebrated balloonist of the pre-war era. Seven of his balloons operated with McClellan's army on the Peninsula. Each balloon had its own hydrogen gas generator and a squad of maintenance men. Messages were relayed by telegraph from balloon observers to forces on the ground. The Confederates, too, managed to make up a balloon using silk dresses donated by ladies of Richmond.

Engineering. In the normal course of a table top battle, engineers have very little or no function but, in a campaign, engineers really come into their own and may well be involved in table top scenarios, perhaps in an assault river crossing or attempting to blow a bridge, etc. The engineers were responsible for the construction of permanent fortifications, building and maintaining lines of communication such as waterways, roads and bridges. The Confederates did not organise a proper engineer corps until 1863.

Chevaux de Frise.

Enclosed gun emplacement.

Revetted breast work with sand bags and gabions.

Siege Craft. By 1863, armies were beginning to dig in. In 1864, both attackers and defenders prepared fieldworks, often of an elaborate nature. As Lee and Johnston retreated in Virginia and Georgia, thousands of slaves directed by engineers and pioneers prepared successive lines of field defences until both armies found themselves forced back to their state capitals which were particularly well protected. These trench systems were not unlike those seen in the First World War. The sides of a trench were revetted with logs and protected by sand bags and earth-filled gabions (wicker baskets). They were traversed so that fields of fire interlocked and often had pits dug in front containing sharpened stakes. Palisades, Chevaux de frise and abatis covered the front of a field work. Bombproof shelters were dug and land

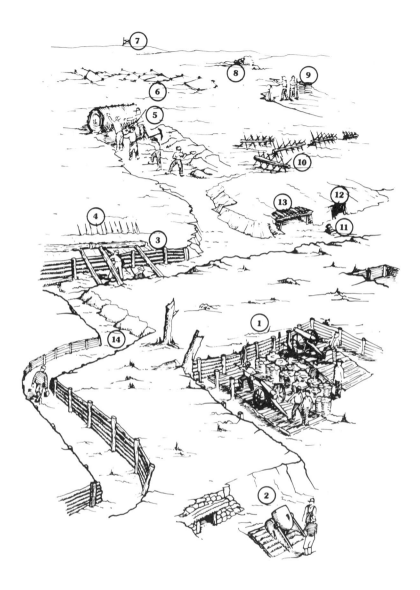

Siege Operations

1. Field battery.
2. Mortar battery.
3. Trench with headlog.
4. Pallisades.
5. Sap head.
6. Cleared copse showing wire strung on tree stumps.
7. Enemy fort.
8. Enemy advanced redoubt.
9. Rifle pit.
10. Chevaux de frise.
11. Trench mortar.
12. Magazine.
13. Bombproof.
14. Communication trench.

mines laid. Mines were usually percussion shells though elec-tronically fired mines were employed (eg Fort Fisher).

Mines were first used at Williamsburg in 1862. Appalled by this 'device of the devil', Union soldiers had captive Confederates dig them all up. Large underground mines were exploded at Vicks-burg and at Petersburg with devastating effect. Earthwork forts were built every 500 yards or so along any line of permanent defence. Outside the main lines were rifle pits and sniper posts, often very close to the enemy. Formal siege tactics followed the classic tradition of parallel lines and zig-zagging saps. Breast-works are easily made from card, filler and cocktail sticks and can really look the part on the wargames table. Trenches are confined to polystyrene or other types of modular terrain.

Miscellaneous. Services such as the medical corps, commissary, ordnance and even sutlers and camp followers can all be represented in a campaign; whilst miscellaneous services to a wargamer, for real armies they were essential. With imagination, such miscellany can find a role in wargames and campaigns in a meaningful way.

8 NAVAL WARFARE

WAR ON THE WATER

Naval Strategies

Federal naval strategy was based around two main objectives. First, the 'Anoconda' Plan, which advocated strangulation of the Confederacy by closing her sea ports and, secondly, control of the Mississippi River. Confederate strategy was based on commerce destruction, and ironclad river and harbour defence. The blockade of the Southern ports gave the Confederacy 'belligerent' status and therefore credibility as an international trader. It took some time for the blockade to take effect. With only fourteen ships available in home waters at the outbreak of the Civil War, it was simply impossible to operate an effective blockade of the 3,500 miles of Southern coastline. The Federal assault on the Mississippi began with the seizure of the South's biggest city, New Orleans, and then Memphis in the first half of 1862. These had been entirely naval victories but the assistance of the army was required to capture the final fortress on the Mississippi, Vicksburg, in July 1863.

The Confederate defence centred around forts which guarded a port, with perhaps several shore batteries also covering the approaches. Without any naval forces at all when the war broke out, the Confederates had to build up their navy from scratch. A heavily casemated ironclad, built upon the hull of an old or salvaged wooden ship, formed the core of the port and river defence system. Because these vessels were few and because they were not always seaworthy even in coastal waters, they were usually held back behind such obstacles as torpedo fields (mine fields), with orders to engage enemy vessels passing through.

Commerce destruction by the seven Confederate cruisers did littlo to alleviate the pressure of the Union blockade, as the Federal Naval Department would not detach ships to hunt thom. The most famous commerce raider, the *Alabama*, was finally sunk off the coast of Cherbourg, France on 19th June, 1864 by the *U.S.S. Kearsarge.* It is probably true to say that if the Union had not possessed 600 or so vessels to the Confederacy's 150, then the North would not have won the war.

Types Of Vessel

As has already been noted, the Confederates relied on one or two forts, backed by a powerful ironclad. Mallory, the Confederate Secretary of the Navy, was innovative in his approach to the changing style of naval warfare. Just before the Civil War, the French had built the first ironclad ship, *Gloire* and the British had soon after countered with the superior *Warrior*. In October 1861, history was made at the Head of the Passes on the Mississippi when, for the first time ever, an ironclad (of the Confederate Navy) engaged an enemy warship. This ironclad was the *Mannassas*.

In March 1862 another Confederate ironclad, the *Virginia*, fought against a Union ironclad, the *Monitor*, in what was the first battle of ironclad ships. The ironclad demonstrated to all the vulnerability of the wooden warship. The *Mannassas* was turtle-shaped and carried a fixed 9 inch gun. The *Virginia* looked like a 'floating barn'; so heavy was its casemate, the decks were actually submerged. Other Confederate ironclads did not tend to sink so far into the water but were based on the *Virginia's* design. The *Monitor*, designed by Ericsson, was an altogether different breed of vessel, but no less strange in appearance; rather like a 'cheese box on a raft'. In fact, the raft part of the ship overhung the hull considerably and consisted of 4½ inch iron plate. The turret revolved and housed two 11 inch Dahlgren (smoothbore) guns, protected by 8 inches of iron plate. The *Monitor* provided the basic design for future coastal ironclads. In action, the monitors covered the wooden vessels which fired heavy broadsides over their decks, safe from being rammed. Ramming was the best way to sink another ship, despite the big guns that were used, and fighting between ironclads took place at point blank ranges in many battles. Some vessels were equipped with special rams, others relied on their armour plated hulls.

On the Western rivers, paddle steamers were converted to gunboats by cladding them with cotton or wood or thin iron plating – 'tin clads'.

The main strength of the Western Flotilla lay in its seven casemated ironclads, built by Eades in late 1861. Since side-paddle wheels could be easily damaged and stern wheels prevented any guns aft, their paddle wheels were built inside the casemates sixty feet forward of their fantails. The flotilla was later augmented by more ironclads of similar design. Mortar boats mounting 13 inch mortars were added to the Western flotilla and the Gulf Squadron to aid in the reduction of forts.

In practice, it was often possible to run past the forts while these were under bombardment rather than after they were reduced. Because of the Confederate success with rams, Ellet added a ram fleet of specially strengthened gunboats to the Western Flotilla. Coastal vessels, such as frigates, mounting about 50 guns and sloops mounting 30 guns, were later used in conjunction with 'monitors' – some of the later types had twin turrets. Monitors had to be used near the coast as heavy seas could cause them to sink; they also had to be towed in transit.

Guns at Sea

Naval artillery was of two types. First, Dalgren or Rodman smoothbores, and secondly Parrott rifles. The 15 inch smooth-bore was the largest calibre in use, but 11 inch and 9 inch guns were more usual. Smaller gunboats carried 30 pounders. All of these guns had ranges over a mile, but under 600 yards was the most effective range against forts and ironclads. The smoothbore guns were used for 'racking' which meant firing heavy balls at low velocity to damage the armour of a ship. The rifles were used for 'punching' which meant penetration of the armour to hit the real target beyond – ie the ship's crew. Although it was not fully appreciated at the time, this sort of fire was more effective.

Rifles fired high velocity elongated shot. The trouble was that the Parrotts had a reputation for bursting. At Fort Fisher, in 1864, every Parrott gun in the fleet burst, causing 45 casualties to the enemy's 11. Rates of fire varied from one round per two to ten minutes depending on the size of gun. Shell and solid shot could be fired from all the naval guns as well as grape shot. When the *Virginia* went out to sink the Union wooden ships in Hampton Roads, she used red-hot shot to set them on fire. Next day, loaded with more appropriate shell, she had the misfortune to encounter the *Monitor*, against which solid shot would have been more effective!

Coastal Defences

Sunken vessels, stakes and torpedoes (mines) were frequently employed to block river approaches. Natural defences, such as sand bars and low water tides, added to and determined the arrangements of defence. Forts were made of stone or brick and many dated back to Revolutionary War times. More modern defences were sand-bagged and earth-banked which deadened the impact of explosive shells. Although reduced to a ruin, Fort Sumter was just as effective at the end of the war as a pile of brick dust as she was when South Carolina troops fired on her in 1861.

Wargames Suggestions

Typical wargame actions will centre on a Union assault on a Confederate port. At 1:1,200 scale, every type of vessel can be represented on table. Forts are available too but can easily be constructed from card. The Union side would possibly have a handful of monitors, rather more screw frigates and a couple of paddle steamers, and perhaps a few mortar boats. Confederate forces would consist of two forts, and/or land batteries, a minefield, river obstacles (eg pilings), a powerful but sluggish ironclad and accompanying wooden-clad gunboats. Riverine actions might involve a Union force of a handful of Eads ironclads, a few later ironclads, one or two wooden gunboats, a few tin clads, several mortar boats and a handful of Ellet rams against several river batteries, a fort, a fleet of wooden, tin and cotton clad gunboats and a powerful ironclad.

Large-scale models can also be effectively used in the Civil War because the ranges at which ironclads duelled could easily be accommodated on an average-sized table. It is not beyond the abilities of the average modeller to construct ironclads from card and these can be used alongside 5mm wargames figures. Skirmish boarding actions can be fought, perhaps based on an actual incident occurring in a 1:1,200 engagement – naval figures and guns are available in 15mm scale.

9 CONCLUSION AND FURTHER READING

Wargaming the American Civil War has come a long way since the original Airfix Civil War figures popularised the period as a cheap and easily obtainable way of getting into wargaming. Today's gamer is well served by a plethora of manufacturers trading in figures, scenics, books and all the other paraphernalia of the hobby. Some exquisite and comprehensive figure lines have been launched onto the market in recent years, confirming the popularity of ACW gaming in the top five of wargames periods. Wargamers have been well served with literature on ACW topics too, of late; in particular, Paddy Griffiths' excellent books *Battle in the Civil War* and *Rally Once Again*. In the Osprey series of books, Philip Katcher has written some fine books specifically on uniforms and equipment which should upgrade the authenticity of wargames figures considerably.

Books of particular interest to wargamers are:

CATTON, B. *The Army of the Potomac* (A trilogy), London, 1951–53. (excellent read).

COGGINS, J. *Arms and Equipment of the Civil War*, Doubleday, 1962. (best of its kind).

COOPER, H. J. *Chancellorsville*, Knights Battles for Wargamers, 1972.

DAVIS, P. & COOPER, H. J. *First Bull Run*, Knights Battles for Wargamers, 1971.

ELTING, J. R. & McAFEE, M. J. (eds) *Long Endure; The Civil War Period* 1852–1867, Cal. 1982.

GRIFFITH, P. *Battle in the Civil War*, Fieldbooks, 1986.

GRIFFITH, P. *Rally Once Again*, Corwood Press, 1987.

GRIFFITH, P. (ed.) *Transactions of the Conference on the Military Aspects of the American Civil War*, Knuston Hall, 1905.

HENDERSON, G. F. R. *Stonewall Jackson*, Longmans, 1961.

HATTAWAY, H. & JONES, A. *How the North Won*, Univ. of Illinois, 1983. (excellent on strategy)

HAZLETT, J. C., OLMSTEAD, E. & PARKS, M. H. *Field Artillery Weapons of the Civil War*, London, 1983.

HOGG, I. V. *Weapons of the American Civil War*, Bison Books, 1987.

JOHNSON, C. & McLAUGHLIN, M. *Battles of the American Civil War*, Sampson Low, 1977.

KATCHER, P. *American Civil War Armies* Vols 1 to 5, Osprey, 1986–89.

The Army of Northern Virginia, Osprey.

The Army of the Potomac, Osprey.

LORD, F. A. *Civil War Collectors Encyclopaedia*, Stackpole, 1963.

MADAUS, M. H. & NEEDHAM, R. D. *The Battle Flags of the Confederate Army of Tennessee*, Wisconsin, 1976.

MACDONALD, J. *Great Battles of the American Civil War*, London, 1988.

McWHINEY, G. & JAMIESON, P. D. *Attack and Die*, Alabama, 1982.

NAISAWALD, L. VAN *Grape & Canister – The Story of the Field Artillery of the Army of the Potomac*, Oxford, 1960.

NOFI, A. A. *The Gettysburg Campaign*, New York, 1986.

STEVENSON, P. D. *American Civil War Army Lists*, Newbury Rules, 1986.

WISE, J. C. *The Long Arm of Lee*, Oxford, 1959.

ZIMMERMANN, R. J. *Unit Organisations of the American Civil War*, R.A.F.M., Ontario, 1982.

FOOTNOTE

As mentioned in the introduction to this book, The Confederate Historical Society's publications have greatly aided me in my research for this book. It is an organisation well worth joining: Details from Mr. A. H. Mowatt, 60 Stroma Way, Glenrothes, Fife, Scotland, KY7 6RD. Finally, no serious student of the war should be without a set of *Battles and Leaders of the Civil War*, 4 Vols, first published 1884, but lately reprinted.

INDEX